Us Citizenship Test Study Guide 2023/2024

By

Anthony Vitale

HERE IS YOU FREE GIFT!

 SCAN HERE TO DOWNLOAD IT

- <u>Boost Test Prep</u>: Complimentary flashcards to enhance your study.
- <u>Quick Review</u>: Easy-to-use for on-the-go learning.
- <u>Full Coverage</u>: Covers all test sections for comprehensive prep.

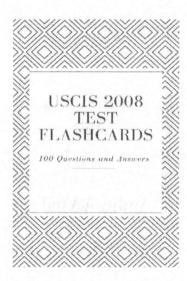

USCIS 2008
TEST
FLASHCARDS

100 Questions and Answers

 SCAN HERE TO DOWNLOAD IT FOR FREE

Table of Contents

Introduction

Becoming a United States citizen is a significant milestone that marks a new chapter in one's life. It is a testament to an individual's commitment to this great nation and its desire to fully participate in its democratic processes. One crucial step in the naturalization process is passing the citizenship test, which assesses applicants' knowledge of American history, government systems, rights, and duties. To assist aspiring citizens in their journey toward achieving this goal, we present the *US Citizenship Test Study Guide 2023/2024*.

The *US Citizenship Test Study Guide 2023/2024* is a comprehensive and meticulously crafted resource designed to provide aspiring citizens with the knowledge and understanding they need to succeed on the citizenship test. It is a valuable tool that equips individuals with the necessary information and insights to navigate the complexities of American citizenship.

This study guide covers a wide range of topics essential to the citizenship test, enabling applicants to understand American history, government, and civic responsibilities deeply. It aims to ensure that applicants not only pass the test but also develop a strong foundation of knowledge that will serve them well as engaged and informed citizens.

Throughout the guide, applicants will find a carefully curated selection of questions that reflect the inquiries they may encounter in the citizenship test. Each question is followed by a clear and concise answer, allowing individuals to verify their understanding and assess their knowledge. Additionally, quick explanations accompany each answer, providing further insights and clarifications to enhance comprehension.

The study guide is structured to provide a systematic approach to learning. It starts by introducing the fundamental concepts of American citizenship, including its rights and duties. It then delves into the naturalization process, explaining the steps involved and guiding applicants through the necessary procedures.

Language proficiency is a vital component of the citizenship test, and Chapter 2 focuses on the English language test. It covers the oral exam, writing test, and reading test, providing examples and tips to help applicants improve their language skills. This chapter aims to enhance applicants' ability to communicate effectively in English, which is crucial for successful integration into American society.

Chapter 3 delves into the civic education test, which evaluates applicants' understanding of American history, government principles, and civic concepts. It covers a wide range of topics, from the principles of American democracy to key historical periods and significant events. This chapter aims to deepen applicants' knowledge of American civics, enabling them to actively participate in the democratic process and make informed decisions as citizens.

As applicants progress through the study guide, they will encounter practical tests of civic education in Chapter 5. These tests allow individuals to apply their knowledge and assess their understanding of the material covered in the previous sections. The questions in this chapter are drawn from both the 2008 and 2020 tests, ensuring applicants are exposed to a comprehensive range of topics and question formats.

This is more than just a preparation tool for the citizenship test. It is a comprehensive resource that fully empowers individuals to embrace their rights and duties as American citizens. By providing a solid foundation of knowledge and understanding, this guide encourages applicants to actively engage in civic life, contribute to their communities, and uphold the values that define the United States.

The US Citizenship Test Study Guide 2023/2024 is a comprehensive and indispensable resource for individuals aspiring to become citizens of the United States. It offers a structured approach to learning, covering the essential topics and concepts necessary for success in the citizenship test. By diligently studying this guide, applicants can embark on their citizenship journey with confidence, knowing that they have the knowledge and understanding needed to fulfill their American dream.

Chapter 1: American Citizenship and Naturalization

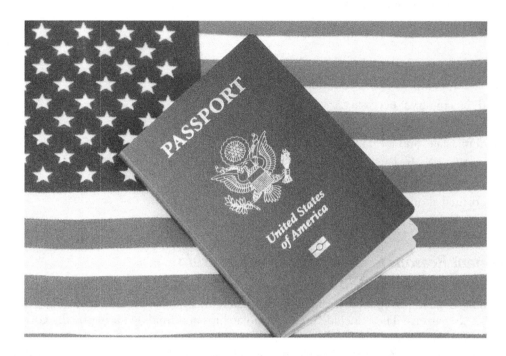

Citizenship is the common thread that binds all Americans to each other. We are a nation bound together by the shared values of liberty, freedom, and equality, not by race or religion.

Over the course of our history, the United States has welcomed new arrivals from around the world. Immigrants have been a part of the shaping and defining of the country we know today. Your contributions are helping to sustain this country's heritage of freedom and opportunity. Naturalized citizens remain an important part of our democracy more than 200 years after our founding. Through citizenship, you, too, will have a voice in the governance of our nation.

The application process is an important decision. Becoming a citizen comes with many benefits and equally important responsibilities. Your application demonstrates your commitment to this country and our form of government.

1.1 Rights and Duties and Economic Opportunity Related to American Citizenship

A number of rights and duties that all citizens are obliged to perform and respect will be laid down in this section. Every citizen has some of their responsibilities laid down by law, but all are vital to the continuation of America's freedom and prosperity.

Rights

1. Freedom in the pursuit of "life, liberty and the pursuit of happiness"

2. Freedom of expression
3. Freedom to worship as you choose
4. The right to apply for federal employment that requires US citizenship
5. The right to a speedy and fair trial by jury
6. The right to run for elected office
7. The right to vote in elections for public officials

Duties

1. Be a participant in the democratic process.
2. Be an active member of your community.
3. Defend the country if necessary.
4. Have respect for the rights, beliefs, and opinions of others.
5. Pay federal, state, and local income and other taxes honestly and on time.
6. Respect and obey the laws of the federal, state, and local governments.
7. Serve on a jury of your peers upon request.
8. Stay informed about issues affecting your community.
9. Support and defend the Constitution.

1.1.1 Important Reasons to Consider U.S. Citizenship

- **Applying for Federal Jobs:** Certain jobs with government agencies require U.S. citizenship.
- **Becoming Eligible for Federal Grants and Scholarships:** Many forms of financial aid are available only to U.S. citizens. These include college scholarships and funds set aside by the government for specific purposes.
- **Becoming an Elected Official:** Citizens are the only ones allowed to run for federal office, namely the US Senate or House of Representatives. Most state and local offices also require citizenship.
- **Bringing Family Members to the U.S.:** U.S. citizens are generally given priority when petitioning to bring family members to this country permanently.
- **Maintaining a Residence:** The right of US citizens to remain in the United States cannot be revoked.
- **Obtaining Government Benefits:** Only U.S. citizens are eligible for some government benefits.
- **Obtaining Citizenship for Children Under 18:** In most instances, a child born abroad to a U.S. citizen is automatically a U.S. citizen.
- **Serving on a Jury:** To serve on a federal jury, you must be a U.S. citizen. U.S. citizens are also the only citizens allowed to serve on juries in most states. For U.S. citizens, serving on a jury is an important responsibility.
- **The Right to Vote:** Only U.S. citizens have voting rights in federal elections. Most states also restrict voting to US citizens in most elections.
- **Travelling with a U.S. Passport:** A U.S. passport allows you to receive assistance from the U.S. government while abroad if needed.

1.1.2 Economic Opportunity for American Citizenship

Many opportunities are only available to U.S. citizens. On this Citizenship Day, we highlight a few of these advantages and motivate qualifying Lawful Permanent Residents (LPRs) to progress towards achieving U.S. citizenship. One significant economic advantage of U.S. citizenship is the potential for higher income. According to a study by the Migration Policy Institute (https://www.migrationpolicy.org/pubs/citizenship-premium.pdf), the average income of citizens is higher than that of green card holders. This is a testament to the economic opportunities that come with U.S. citizenship.

1. Protection from Deportation

Attaining U.S. citizenship provides you and your offspring with immunity from expulsion. As a lawful permanent resident (LPR), specific criminal charges can lead to potential expulsion, and certain behaviors expose Permanent residents to the risk of enduring severe implications like deportation.

2. Citizenship for Your Children

Minors under 18, who are legitimate permanent residents, spontaneously acquire U.S. citizenship when their parents complete the naturalization process. This is truly a gift from parents to their children, as individuals cannot apply for naturalization until they turn 18.

3. Family Reunification

U.S. citizens have the privilege of submitting immigration petitions to the government with the intent of reuniting with their family members. Unlike LPRs, who can only petition for a spouse, minor children, and adult children who aren't married, U.S. citizens have the additional advantage of petitioning for other family members like parents, siblings, and adult children who are married.

4. Eligibility for Government Jobs

Some jobs, such as those in the federal government, are open only to U.S. citizens. In addition, naturalization recipients, on average, do better economically than noncitizens. As a group, they earn 50 to 70 percent more than noncitizens, are more likely to be employed, and are less likely to live below the poverty line. As a direct result of better job preparation, better job matches, and greater ability to change jobs, new citizens could also see individual earnings increases of 8 to 11 percent.

5. Freedom to Travel

LPRs are limited in the amount of time they can travel in a given year. U.S. citizens have the liberty to journey without being subject to these limitations. They also have the option, in the event of a personal crisis or civil unrest, to seek the assistance and protection of U.S. embassies and consulates abroad.

6. Ability to Vote

The right to vote is another benefit of U.S. citizenship. Only U.S. Citizens are empowered to choose the leaders they believe will best represent them, their families, and the communities in which they live.

Other Benefits

Many other benefits come with U.S. citizenship. LPRs do not have the same access to public benefits as citizens, even though they live, work, and pay taxes here. LPRs may be required to pay high premiums for some public benefits and programs, such as Medicare. Citizenship ensures equal access to benefits that are critically important to the elderly and people with disabilities.

Many immigrants feel a strong sense of attachment to their country of origin. U.S. citizenship does not have to be a loss of one's heritage. In fact, many countries even allow dual citizenship, which means you can maintain your status both where you come from and in the United States.

On Citizenship Day and throughout the year, partners of the New Americans Campaign across the country are helping LPRs realize their dream of becoming citizens and achieving a more secure and successful status in the United States.

1.2 How to Obtain Citizenship: Naturalization

Citizenship is the process by which people who have immigrated to the United States of America can become American citizens. Only certain immigrants are eligible: those who have either held a Green Card (legal permanent resident) for 3 to 5 years or those who have served in the military and meet certain requirements.

What is Citizenship?

Citizenship is the designation awarded to an individual born to a U.S. Citizen or to someone who has effectively navigated the naturalization process. Becoming a U.S. citizen comes with many benefits and responsibilities.

Naturalization Timeline

The naturalization process, from the time you submit your application to the time you take the oath of allegiance, currently takes 8–13 months.

Naturalization Costs

The present state application fee for naturalization is $725, which is divided into $640 for processing costs and $85 for biometric services. Military applicants are exempt from both the filing fee and the biometrics fee. Applicants who have reached the age of 75 or more are not required to pay the biometrics fee.

Naturalization Eligibility

The eligibility for naturalization is usually determined by several factors, such as.

- How long have you been in possession of your green card?
- How long you've physically lived in the U.S.?
- Your service history in the U.S. military, and if applicable, whether your term of service was during "peacetime" or "wartime"

Eligibility to Apply for U.S. Citizenship

If you fall into one of the following categories and have resided in the U.S. for the specified duration, you can apply for naturalization:

1. If you are a green card holder without any special circumstances, you've resided physically in the U.S. for a minimum of 30 months (2.5 years) before you are eligible to apply, and this requirement can be met after 5 years.
2. If you are a green card holder who is married to a U.S. citizen, you need to have physically lived in the U.S. for 18 months (1.5 years) before you can apply, and this requirement can be met after 3 years.
3. In case you're the surviving spouse of a U.S. citizen who passed away while serving honorably in the military, there is no specific duration of residence required, and you can apply for naturalization at any time.
4. If you are a holder of a green card with at least one year of peacetime military service, there is no specific duration of residence required. You can apply for naturalization while on active duty or within 6 months of being honorably discharged from the military.
5. If you are a green card holder having less than 1 year of peacetime military service, you must have physically lived in the U.S. for at least 30 months (2.5 years) before you can apply, and this requirement can be met after 5 years.
6. If you are a holder of a green card with at least one year of peacetime military service and have been honorably discharged from the military more than 6 months ago, you must have physically lived in the United States for at least 30 months (2.5 years) before you can apply, and this requirement can be met after 5 years.
7. If you are a military member with any period of wartime service (with or without a green card), there is no specific duration of residence required, and you can apply for naturalization at any time.

8. Consecutive or not, any period of military service counts as being physically present in the United States.
9. A discharge marked "General, Under Honorable Conditions" is considered an "honorable" discharge for naturalization purposes.

If you are a green card holder, you have at least five years after receiving your green card to apply for U.S. citizenship without any special circumstances. You must also have physically lived in the United States for at least 30 months (two and a half years) of those five years.

If you have been married to a United States citizen for no less than three years and have lived with your spouse during that time, you can apply to become a US citizen at least three years after receiving your green card. You must also have been physically present in the United States for at least 18 months (one and a half years) of those three years. Your spouse must have lived in the United States for at least three years.

If you're the widow or widower of a US citizen who died during honorable service in the US military (and you were living with them at the time of their death), as long as you have a green card at the point of your citizenship interview, you can apply for US citizenship at any time. There is no requirement that you have been a green card holder for a certain number of years or have physically resided in the United States for a certain number of months prior to the application.

You can apply at any time, and you don't have to be a green card holder if you served in the U.S. military during a time of war. You (or your military spouse) only need to be physically present in the United States (including US territories) or on a US vessel at the time of enlistment, re-enlistment, extension of service, or induction into the military. It is not necessary to hold a green card for a certain number of years (if any) or to be a physical resident of the U.S. for a certain number of months before applying for citizenship.

1.2.1 Naturalization Requirements

In addition to waiting 3 or 5 years after you receive your green card (unless you're applying on the basis of qualifying military service), you must also meet the following requirements to proceed with the naturalization process to become a citizen of the United States:
1. You must be 18 years of age or older.
2. During the three- or five-year waiting period, you must not have traveled outside the United States for six months or more.
3. You must have resided for at least three months in the State where you wish to become a naturalized citizen.
4. You must be of "good moral character," which is generally defined as character measured by the standards of average citizens in your community. More concretely, it means that at no time prior to applying for naturalization has your record contained certain types of felonies such as murder, illegal gambling, or deliberately lying to the government to gain immigration advantages and that you've not lied during your naturalization interview. The government's determination of an applicant's compliance with this requirement will be on a case-by-case basis.
5. You must pass two tests: one in English, which tests your ability to write, read, and speak English, and one in civics, which tests your knowledge of American history and government.
6. You must be willing to serve in the United States military or provide civilian service to the United States if requested.
7. You must register with the Selective Service System if you are a man and have lived in the USA while you were between the ages of 18 and 25.
8. You must be willing to defend the Constitution of the United States.

Exceptions Based on Age and Disability

- Exception: Applicants aged 50 and older who have been residents in the United States for at least twenty years as green card holders are exempt from the English test, but they are still required to take the civics test.
- Exception: Applicants aged 55 and older who have been residents in the United States for at least 15 years as green card holders are exempt from the English test, but they are still required to take the civics test.
- Exception: Applicants aged 65 and older who have been residents in the United States for at least twenty years as a green card holder are exempt from the English test, and they are also exempt from the majority of the civics test. Instead of answering 100 questions, they only need to study 20 questions. During the test, the applicant will be asked ten questions and must answer no fewer than six correctly to pass.
- Exception: Applicants with a medical disability that is expected to last at least 12 months can be exempt from both the English test and the civics test, but this exemption requires an approved waiver.

Disability Exceptions

Applicants with a physical, developmental, or intellectual disability may be exempt from the English language proficiency and civics test requirements listed above. You may apply for a waiver by submitting Form N-648 ("Medical Certification for Disability Exceptions"). This form must be completed by a physician.

Exemptions Based on Peacetime Military Service

Individuals are exempt from requirements 2 and 3 above if they are applying for naturalization based on at least one year of peacetime military service. The applicant's criminal record must be free of certain felonies for at least five years prior to application and up to the time of naturalization to meet requirement #4.

Exceptions Based on Wartime Military Service

Individuals are exempt from requirements #1 (they can be any age), #2, and #3 above if they are applying for naturalization based on any period of wartime military service. The applicant's criminal record must be free of certain felonies for at least one year prior to the application and up to the time of naturalization to meet requirement #4.

Special Requirements for U.S. Military Personnel

For holders of a green card who are current or former U.S. military personnel, there are additional requirements:

- You must not have deserted (left before getting discharged) from the U.S. Military.
- You must never have received a discharge or exemption from the US military based on your status as a non-citizen.

What if I can't afford the filing fee?

If you cannot afford the filing fee due to income limitations, you may be eligible for a fee reduction or waiver.

1.3 The Naturalization Process

The process of becoming a U.S. citizen is known as naturalization. The United States Citizenship and Immigration Services (USCIS) has outlined a 10-step process for naturalization, which is detailed below:

1.3.1 Check if You Are Already a Citizen

Before beginning the naturalization process, it's important to determine if you are already a U.S. citizen. This can occur if you were born in the United States or certain territories or outlying possessions of the United States, or if you were born to U.S. citizen parents, depending on the laws in effect at the time of your birth. You could also acquire citizenship through your parents after your birth but before the age of 18.

1.3.2 Check if You Are Eligible to Become a Citizen

To be eligible for naturalization, you must meet several requirements. These include being at least 18 years old at the time of filing, being a permanent resident (green card holder) for at least five years (or three years if married to a U.S. citizen), demonstrating continuous residence and physical presence in the United States, and showing good moral character, among other requirements.

1.3.3 Prepare the N-400 Form

Part 1. Information About Your Eligibility *(Check only one box or your Form N-400 may be delayed)*	Enter Your 9 Digit A-Number: ▶ A-

You are at least 18 years old **and**

1. ☐ Have been a Permanent Resident of the United States for at least 5 years.

2. ☒ Have been a Permanent Resident of the United States for at least 3 years. In addition, you have been married to and living with the same U.S. citizen spouse for the last 3 years, **and** your spouse has been a U.S. citizen for the last 3 years at the time of filing your Form N-400.

3. ☐ Are a Permanent Resident of the United States, and you are the spouse of a U.S. citizen, **and** your U.S. citizen spouse is regularly engaged in specified employment abroad. *(Section 319(b) of the Immigration and Nationality Act)*

4. ☐ Are applying on the basis of qualifying military service.

5. ☐ Other (explain):

The N-400 form, also known as the Application for Naturalization, is the form used to apply for U.S. citizenship. It requires detailed information about your background, including your residence and employment history, marital history, and information about any children you may have. It also includes questions about your moral character and your commitment to the Constitution of the United States.

1.3.4 Submit the N-400 Form and Pay the Fees

Once you've completed the N-400 form, you must submit it to USCIS along with the necessary supporting documents and the appropriate fees. At the time this book was written the application fee was $640, and the biometric services fee was $85, but these fees are subject to change, so it's important to check the current fees on the USCIS website.

1.3.5 Biometrics Appointment

The next step is to schedule your biometric appointment—basically, to have your fingerprints taken—at your local USCIS field office. During the naturalization process, USCIS will take your fingerprints to conduct a background check, just as they do during the family-based green card process. Your fingerprinting appointment will usually take place about one month after the USCIS receives your application for U.S. citizenship.

1.3.6 USCIS Officer Exam and Interview
The Interview

The Citizenship Interview is usually scheduled to take place about 14 months after you apply to become a U.S. citizen. However, the exact amount of time it will take for your naturalization application to be processed is highly dependent on the USCIS field office that is handling your case, which will be assigned to you as per your zip code.

During the naturalization interview, a USCIS officer will verify that all of the information provided on your naturalization application is correct and complete. The interview will usually take place at the USCIS office closest to you. If you are applying from abroad, you will visit a U.S. Embassy or Consulate to get interviewed. If you are on active duty in the military, your naturalization interview may be held at a military installation or facility.

The Exam

The citizenship interview is called a "citizenship exam" because the USCIS officer will also give you a two-part citizenship test (unless you qualify for a waiver): The first component, an English language test, is an assessment of your English language skills in writing and speaking. The second, a civics test, is an assessment of your knowledge of U.S. history and basic information about the workings of the U.S. government.

But don't worry about it! These tests are fairly easy, and the USCIS will provide you with study materials for your preparation. You will be provided with two opportunities to take the tests. The first chance will be during your interview, and if needed, you will have another opportunity at a later date to retake any section of the test that you were unable to pass initially.

If you pass the interview and the exam, the USCIS Officer will approve your application when the interview ends. In some cases, the USCIS officer may ask you to provide additional documentation or schedule a second interview.

If you do not pass the interview, USCIS will send you a letter explaining the grounds for the denial, but you have 30 days from the date of receipt of the letter to appeal their decision or to reapply. A USCIS policy on denied applications emphasizes the importance of completing the naturalization application correctly the first time and meeting all requirements, which went into effect on September 11, 2018.

1.3.7 USCIS Decision on Application

After the interview, USCIS will make a decision on your application. They may either grant, continue, or deny your application. If your application is granted, you have been approved for naturalization. If your application is continued, it means USCIS needs additional evidence or documentation, or you need to pass additional tests. If your application is denied, it means USCIS has determined you are not eligible for naturalization.

1.3.8 Oath

You are almost at the end of the process! Once your application is approved, you will be part of an oath of allegiance ceremony. It's very important that you complete this step. Until you take the Oath of Allegiance, you are not a U.S. citizen.

After your naturalization interview, you'll receive a notice in the mail with the time, date, and location of the ceremony. The location is usually a local courthouse or USCIS office. The length of time between your citizenship interview and the ceremony will vary from state to state.

You'll have to have your green card returned to you at the time of check-in. Once the Ceremony is over, you'll receive your Certificate of Naturalization and get to start living as a U.S. Citizen!

Benefits of Naturalization

Once you've received your certificate of naturalization, you'll be able to access a number of benefits that weren't previously available to you as a Green Card holder. In this section, we'll discuss some of them.

- **Voting Rights:** Green card holders may only be able to vote in certain local elections, but with naturalization, they can impact the national stage and vote in federal elections.
- **Eligibility to Run for Office:** To be eligible to run for office in U.S. elections, you must be a citizen, which means that with a Certificate of Naturalization, you can run for office.
- **No more Immigration Forms:** In the future, you won't have to go through the hassle of filing immigration forms with the USCIS. That means you won't have to pay the filing fee, renew or replace your Green Card, and you won't need to keep in contact with the United States government if you decide to move.
- **New Employment Opportunities:** Only U.S. citizens can be hired to work for the U.S. government, according to U.S. law. Federal employees generally receive higher salaries and benefits than their private-sector counterparts, although income levels vary.
- **Greater Access to Government Assistance Programs:** As a holder of green card, you have limited, if any, access to federal programs such as Social Security and Medicare. But with a Certificate of Naturalization, you'll no longer face these restrictions. In some cases, you may even be eligible for federal college aid reserved for U.S. citizens.
- **No More Deportations:** You cannot be forcibly removed from the United States, just like any other U.S. citizen. This is true even if you have a criminal conviction or are under arrest. The only way to deport a citizen is to revoke his or her citizenship, which is rarely done. For this to happen, the original application would have to have been fraudulent in some way.
- **Ability To Sponsor Relatives Seeking Immigration Status:** With a Certificate of Naturalization, you can sponsor any sibling, parent, or adult child who wishes to apply for lawful permanent residence in the United States.
- **Automatic Citizenship for Children:** Once you're naturalized, your children automatically become citizens. This applies even if they were born abroad. Be sure to notify the U.S. consulate or embassy if your child is born outside the United States.

The Power of the U.S. Passport

As a citizen of the United States, you're entitled to a U.S. passport. There are many benefits to having a U.S. passport. For starters, you have visa-free access to more than 180 countries and territories around the world. And if you have an emergency while you're abroad, you can contact the local U.S. consulate or embassy for help. Since the U.S. government places no restrictions on the duration or frequency of international travel, you'll have almost complete freedom to travel the globe. (Note: It's always a good idea to check the specific visa requirements for a particular country before you make any travel arrangements).

Special Considerations

Before you get started on becoming a U.S. citizen, it's important to understand the basic responsibilities that come with being an American citizen. Some of the most important of these responsibilities are listed below:

Renunciation of citizenship: You may have to renounce your citizenship in other countries. You may be required to give up your current citizenship when you become an American, depending on your home country's rules regarding dual citizenship (holding citizenship in two countries at the same time). The United States allows dual citizenship. However, when traveling in and out of the United States, US citizens are required to carry a U.S. passport.

Many countries—Australia, Canada, and the United Kingdom, for example—also allow you to be a citizen of another country. However, once you become an American citizen, India, Japan, and some other countries require you to give up your citizenship in those countries.

If you intend to keep your citizenship in your home country, it's best to check its policy on dual citizenship before applying for naturalization.

Military service: You may be required to serve in the military. Military conscription has been an official policy of the United States since the end of the Vietnam War in 1973. However, if the draft were to be reinstated, you could be subject to conscription. You must register with the Selective Service System if you are a U.S. citizen or green card holder and have lived in the U.S. between the ages of 18 and 25.

Jury Duty: You may be required to serve on a jury. In the United States, it is mandatory to serve on a jury in a court of law. If you are summoned for jury duty, you must be there. Only those who are selected by the judge and the attorneys after they have been summoned will actually serve on the jury.

Exempted from federal jury duty are members of the military on active duty, professional firefighters and police officers, and some government employees who serve full-time in their positions. Generally, it is possible to request an exemption from service for persons who served in the past 2 years on a federal jury, are over 71 years of age, or are volunteers first responders. However, policies vary from district court to district court. State and local courts have their own rules, but they generally also exempt individuals on the basis of age, disability, or because of their position in a public office.

Paying Taxes: No matter where you live, you must file U.S. income tax returns for the rest of your life. If you are an expatriate, you still have to report your income to the US tax authorities. You can, however, exclude as much of your income as the U.S. government permits each year, which is currently over $100,000, provided you meet certain requirements. This means it won't be taxed. Any income in excess of this limit will generally be subject to tax.

Criminal History: Your criminal history will be the subject of very close scrutiny. Seeking legal counsel before applying for naturalization is crucial, particularly if you have engaged in activities that could result in deportation, such as immigration fraud, drug abuse, or domestic violence.

Chapter 2: The Test: How It is Structured

2.1 The English Language Test: The Oral Exam, Writing Test, and Reading Test

The English Language Test is an essential component of the naturalization process for individuals seeking U.S. citizenship. It is designed to assess an applicant's ability to speak, listen, read, and write in the English language. Proficiency in English is crucial for effective communication, integration into American society, and participation in various aspects of daily life. In this section, we will explore the details of the English Language Test, including its purpose, structure, and evaluation criteria.

Purpose of the English Language Test

The primary objective of the English Language Test is to ensure that applicants have a sufficient level of English proficiency to engage in meaningful interactions within the United States. By demonstrating their ability to communicate effectively, applicants show their readiness to navigate daily life, understand important information, interact with government officials, and participate fully in the civic and social fabric of the country.

Structure of the English Language Test

The English Language Test consists of three main components: the Oral Exam, the Reading Test, and the Writing Test. Each component evaluates different language skills, providing a comprehensive assessment of an applicant's English proficiency.

2.1.1 The Oral Exam

The Oral Exam is designed to assess an applicant's ability to speak and understand spoken English. During the exam, a USCIS officer engages in a conversation with the applicants to evaluate their fluency, pronunciation, comprehension, and ability to respond appropriately to questions and prompts.

The conversation may cover various topics related to personal background, family, work, hobbies, and general interests. The USCIS officer assesses the applicant's ability to comprehend and provide relevant information using appropriate grammar, vocabulary, and sentence structure.

Format and Requirements

The Oral Exam evaluates the applicant's spoken English proficiency in everyday situations. It allows the USCIS officer to assess the applicant's ability to communicate effectively and demonstrates their readiness to engage with English-speaking individuals and communities in the United States.

To ensure fairness and consistency in the evaluation process, USCIS officers follow established guidelines and use standardized evaluation criteria to assess an applicant's performance during the Oral Exam.

It is important for applicants to prepare for the Oral Exam by practicing their conversational skills, pronunciation, and comprehension. USCIS provides study materials, resources, and sample questions to help applicants familiarize themselves with the type of questions they may encounter during the exam. Additionally, applicants can utilize English language learning resources, language courses, and communication partners to improve their language skills and gain confidence in their ability to communicate effectively.

Evaluation Criteria

During the English Language Test, USCIS officers assess applicants based on a set of evaluation criteria to determine their English language proficiency. The criteria focus on various aspects of language skills, including:

a. Fluency and Coherence: USCIS officers evaluate an applicant's ability to speak with fluency and coherence. This involves the smooth and natural flow of speech, appropriate pace, and clarity of expression. Applicants should aim to articulate their thoughts clearly and express ideas in a logical and organized manner.

b. Vocabulary and Grammar: The applicant's vocabulary and grammar usage are evaluated to assess their command of the English language. A diverse range of vocabulary, accurate word choice, and grammatically correct sentences are essential for effective communication.

c. Pronunciation: USCIS officers assess the applicant's pronunciation to determine their ability to be understood by others. Clear and accurate pronunciation, including correct stress, intonation, and sound production, is crucial for effective spoken communication.

d. Comprehension: The applicant's ability to understand spoken English is evaluated during the Oral Exam. This includes comprehending questions, prompts, and information the UCIS officer provides. Applicants should demonstrate their understanding by responding appropriately and providing relevant information.

e. Interaction and Responsiveness: USCIS officers assess the applicant's ability to engage in a conversation, actively listen, and respond appropriately. Applicants should demonstrate their ability to ask and answer questions, seek clarification when needed, and actively participate in the conversation.

USCIS officers use these evaluation criteria to assess an applicant's English language proficiency during the Oral Exam. Applicants are evaluated based on their individual performance, and there is no predetermined passing score. Instead, officers consider the overall quality of the applicant's language skills and their ability to communicate effectively in English.

Preparation for the English Language Test

Preparing for the English Language Test is crucial to ensure success during the naturalization process. Applicants are encouraged to dedicate time and effort to improve their English language skills and gain confidence in their ability to communicate effectively.

Here are some strategies and tips to help applicants prepare for the English Language Test:

a. **Engage in immersion:** Immersing oneself in an English-speaking environment can greatly enhance language skills. This can include watching English-language movies and TV shows, listening to English podcasts or music, and talking with native English speakers. Immersion allows individuals to familiarize themselves with the natural flow of spoken English, improve vocabulary, and develop an ear for pronunciation.

b. **Practice speaking:** Regular practice is essential for developing speaking skills. Applicants can practice speaking English by conversing with friends, language exchange partners, or language tutors. It is important to focus on fluency, pronunciation, and the ability to express ideas clearly.

c. **Improve vocabulary and grammar:** Building a strong vocabulary and understanding grammar rules are vital for effective communication. Applicants can enhance their vocabulary by reading books, newspapers, and online articles in English. It is also helpful to engage in activities that involve writing, such as journaling, to practice grammar and sentence structure.

d. **Use study materials:** USCIS provides study materials and resources specifically designed to help applicants prepare for the English Language Test. These materials include sample questions, vocabulary lists, and study guides that cover the topics and language skills assessed during the exam. To understand the format and content of the examination, applicants should take advantage of these resources.

e. **Seek professional guidance:** Language courses, tutors, and conversation partners can provide valuable guidance and support in improving English language skills. Working with professionals who specialize in teaching English as a second language can offer personalized instruction and feedback to address specific areas of improvement.

By following these preparation strategies and dedicating time to language practice, applicants can enhance their English language proficiency and increase their chances of success during the English Language Test.

To ensure that applicants have the necessary skills for effective communication within the United States of America, an ESL test is also part of the naturalization process. The Oral Exam evaluates an applicant's ability to speak and understand spoken English, emphasizing fluency, pronunciation, comprehension, and interactive skills. By preparing adequately, utilizing study materials, and engaging in language practice, applicants can improve their English language proficiency and confidently navigate the naturalization process.

It is important to note that USCIS guidelines and requirements may change over time. Therefore, applicants should consult official USCIS resources and seek professional advice to ensure they have the most up-to-date and accurate information regarding the English Language Test. Additionally, applicants should be aware of any additional language requirements that may exist at the state or local level, as these can vary.

Developing English language skills facilitates the naturalization process and opens doors to better integration, communication, and opportunities in the United States. Through dedication, practice, and a commitment to language learning, applicants can successfully navigate the English Language Test and embark on their journey toward U.S. citizenship.

2.1.2 The Writing Test

The Writing Test is an important component of the U.S. naturalization process, designed to assess an applicant's ability to write in English. It evaluates the applicant's proficiency in written communication, including grammar, sentence structure, vocabulary usage, and overall clarity of expression. The test aims to ensure that individuals seeking citizenship possess the necessary skills to effectively communicate in written English, as it is a vital aspect of daily life, work, and civic engagement in the United States.

Format and Requirements

The Writing Test consists of a writing prompt that the applicant must respond to by writing a sentence or a short paragraph. The prompt typically requires the applicant to demonstrate their understanding of a specific concept or provide a personal response related to U.S. history, government, or civic values.

The applicant's response must be written in English using correct grammar, punctuation, and capitalization. Handwriting is also evaluated, although legibility is more important than calligraphy or artistic presentation.

Evaluation Criteria

USCIS officers assess the applicant's writing proficiency based on several criteria:

a. **Language Proficiency:** The applicant's ability to use appropriate vocabulary, grammar, and sentence structure is evaluated. The response should demonstrate a command of English language conventions, including proper use of tenses, subject-verb agreement, word choice, and sentence coherence.

b. **Clarity and Coherence:** The applicant's writing should convey the intended message clearly and effectively. The response should be organized, with ideas presented in a logical sequence. Cohesive devices, such as transitional words and phrases, can connect thoughts and ensure coherence.

c. **Content and Relevance:** The applicant's response should address the prompt comprehensively and provide relevant information. It is important to stay focused on the topic and provide accurate and appropriate details that support the main idea. Tangential or unrelated information should be avoided.

d. **Length and Structure:** While there is no specific word count requirement for the Writing Test, applicants must provide a sufficient and meaningful response. A concise and well-structured answer is preferred over a lengthy and disorganized one.

e. **Spelling and Punctuation:** The applicant's ability to spell words correctly and use proper punctuation is assessed. Attention to detail is important to ensure accuracy and clarity in written communication.

Preparation for the Writing Test

Adequate preparation is essential to perform well on the Writing Test. Here are some tips to help applicants prepare:

a. **Practice writing in English:** Regular writing practice can enhance proficiency. Applicants should dedicate time to writing in English on various topics, focusing on grammar, vocabulary, and clarity of expression. It is beneficial to seek feedback from English-speaking peers, tutors, or instructors to identify areas for improvement.

b. **Expand vocabulary:** Building a robust vocabulary is crucial for effective written communication. Applicants can improve their vocabulary by reading English literature, newspapers, and online articles. They should make a habit of noting down unfamiliar words and their meanings and incorporating them into their writing.

c. **Study grammar and sentence structure:** Understanding and applying grammar rules is essential for producing coherent and error-free writing. Applicants should review grammar resources, such as textbooks, online tutorials, or language learning apps, to reinforce their knowledge of grammar and sentence structure.

d. **Manage your time:** The Writing Test is typically time-limited. Practicing writing within a specified time frame can help applicants develop the ability to organize their thoughts quickly and express them concisely. It is advisable to practice writing within a given time limit to simulate the test conditions.

e. **Seek Professional Assistance:** Working with an English language tutor or taking writing classes can provide valuable guidance and feedback. Tutors or instructors can identify areas of improvement, offer personalized instruction, and provide constructive criticism to enhance writing skills.

Tips for the Writing Test

When taking the Writing Test, applicants should keep the following tips in mind:

a. **Read the prompt carefully:** Before starting to write, applicants should thoroughly understand the prompt. They should pay attention to the question being asked and any specific instructions or requirements provided. It is important to address all aspects of the prompt in the response.

b. **Plan and organize:** Taking a few moments to plan the response can improve the organization and coherence of the writing. Applicants can outline their main points or create a brief structure before writing. This helps in ensuring a clear and logical flow of ideas.

c. **Focus on clarity and accuracy:** Clear communication is essential. Applicants should prioritize conveying their message accurately and understandably. While vocabulary and sentence structure are important, it is crucial to prioritize clarity over complexity. Using simpler language and structures that applicants are confident with is preferable to attempting overly complicated language and risking errors.

d. **Proofread and edit:** Applicants should allocate time in the end to review their responses. Proofreading allows for the identification and correction of spelling mistakes, punctuation errors, and grammatical inaccuracies. Applicants should ensure their writing is coherent and cohesive, making any necessary revisions before submitting their response.

e. **Stay calm and focused:** It is natural to feel nervous during the Writing Test, but it is important to remain calm and focused. Anxiety can hinder performance, so applicants should take deep breaths, concentrate on the task at hand, and trust in their preparation.

The Writing Test is a significant part of the U.S. naturalization process, evaluating an applicant's ability to write in English. By demonstrating proficiency in written communication, applicants prove their readiness to engage effectively in various aspects of American life, including work, education, and civic participation. Adequate preparation, practice, and attention to language proficiency, clarity, and coherence are key to performing well on the Writing Test. With dedicated effort and commitment, applicants can master the skills required to complete this crucial step toward U.S. citizenship.

2.1.3 The Reading Test

The Reading Test is an essential component of the U.S. naturalization process, designed to assess an applicant's ability to read and understand English. It evaluates the applicant's proficiency in reading comprehension, vocabulary recognition, and the ability to glean information from written passages. The test aims to ensure that individuals seeking U.S. citizenship have the necessary reading skills to access and comprehend information relevant to daily life, civic responsibilities, and engagement in the United States.

Format and Requirements

The Reading Test consists of three to four reading passages, each followed by several multiple-choice questions. The passages cover various topics related to U.S. history, government, and civic values. The questions assess the applicant's ability to comprehend the content, draw logical inferences, and identify specific details.

Evaluation Criteria

USCIS officers evaluate the applicant's reading proficiency based on several criteria:

a. **Comprehension:** The applicant's ability to understand the main ideas and details presented in the passages is assessed. Comprehension involves identifying the central theme, understanding the sequence of events, and recognizing the purpose of the text.

b. **Vocabulary Recognition:** The applicant's familiarity with English vocabulary is tested through exposure to words commonly used in everyday life and civic contexts. Recognition of relevant terms and phrases is crucial for understanding the passages and answering the questions accurately.

c. **Logical Inferences:** The applicant's capacity to draw logical inferences from the information presented in the passages is evaluated. This skill requires making reasonable conclusions based on the given content.

d. **Contextual Understanding:** The applicant's capability to understand the meaning of words and phrases in context is assessed. This skill is important for comprehending unfamiliar vocabulary encountered in reading passages.

e. **Ability to Analyze Information:** The applicant's capacity to identify specific details and factual information in the passages is tested. This skill involves locating relevant information to answer the multiple-choice questions accurately.

Preparation for the Reading Test

Adequate preparation is crucial to perform well on the Reading Test. Here are some tips to help applicants prepare:

a. Reading Practice: Regularly reading in English is essential to improve reading comprehension skills. Applicants should engage with a variety of texts, such as newspapers, magazines, online articles, and books. This practice exposes them to diverse writing styles, topics, and vocabulary.

b. Vocabulary Development: Building a strong vocabulary is key to understanding the reading passages. Applicants can learn new words by using dictionaries, flashcards, and vocabulary-building apps. Understanding word roots, prefixes, and suffixes can also help decipher the meanings of unfamiliar words.

c. Analyzing Texts: While reading, applicants should practice summarizing the main ideas and identifying key details. Analyzing the structure and purpose of different texts helps enhance reading comprehension abilities.

d. Practice with Sample Tests: USCIS provides sample reading tests on their official website, which applicants can use for practice. Taking these sample tests under timed conditions can help simulate the actual test environment and improve time management skills.

e. Seek Assistance and Feedback: Working with a tutor or language instructor can provide valuable guidance and feedback. Tutors can help identify areas of improvement and suggest specific strategies to enhance reading comprehension skills.

Tips for the Reading Test

When taking the Reading Test, applicants should consider the following tips:

a. **Read carefully and thoroughly:** Applicants should read each passage carefully, paying attention to the main ideas and supporting details. Skimming or skipping portions may lead to misunderstandings and inaccuracies in answering the questions.

b. **Analyze the questions:** Before attempting to answer the questions, applicants should analyze them to understand what information they need to find in the passage. This approach helps focus attention and avoid distractions.

c. **Identify keywords:** Identifying keywords and phrases in the questions and passages can assist in locating the relevant information needed to answer the questions correctly.

d. **Use the process of elimination:** If uncertain about an answer, applicants can use the process of elimination to narrow down the options. By eliminating clearly incorrect choices, the chances of selecting the correct answer improve.

e. **Manage time effectively:** Time management is crucial during the Reading Test. Applicants should allocate sufficient time to read the passages, understand the questions, and answer them accurately. Practicing under timed conditions can help develop this skill.

The Reading Test is vital in assessing an applicant's reading comprehension skills as part of the U.S. naturalization process. By demonstrating proficiency in reading English, applicants prove their ability to understand important civic information, participate in American society, and make informed decisions as citizens. Through dedicated practice, vocabulary development, and exposure to various texts, applicants can enhance their reading abilities and perform well on the Reading Test. Taking the time to prepare adequately and implement effective strategies will contribute to a successful outcome on this crucial step toward U.S. citizenship.

2.2 The Civics Test: A Comparison of the 2008 and 2020 Versions and Choosing Between the Two Tests

The Civics Test is a crucial component of the naturalization process in the United States. It evaluates applicants' knowledge and understanding of American government, history, and civic principles. The test ensures that individuals seeking to become citizens possess the necessary knowledge to fully engage in civic life, exercise their rights and responsibilities, and contribute to the democratic fabric of the nation.

The Civics Test consists of a set of questions and answers covering various topics, including principles of American democracy, the U.S. government system, rights and duties of citizens, and significant events in American history. It serves as a tool to assess applicants' familiarity with the foundations and workings of the United States, ensuring that they have a comprehensive understanding of the nation's values, systems, and history.

2.2.1 The 2008 Version

The 2008 version of the Civics Test is an integral part of the naturalization process in the United States. It consists of 100 questions that assess an applicant's knowledge of American government, history, and civic principles. By examining an individual's understanding of these essential aspects, the test ensures they are well-informed and prepared to become active and engaged citizens.

The questions in the 2008 version cover a broad range of topics, including the principles of American democracy, the governance system, the rights and duties of citizens, and significant historical events. Let's explore some key aspects of the 2008 Civics Test:

Question Format

The questions in the 2008 Civics Test are multiple-choice. Each question has four possible answer options, and the applicant must select the correct answer. The purpose of this format is to evaluate the applicant's knowledge and understanding of various aspects of American government and history.

Content Coverage

The questions in the 2008 Civics Test cover a wide array of topics related to American civics. These include principles such as separation of powers, the rule of law, and checks and balances. The governance system questions delve into the structure and functions of the three branches of government: the executive, legislative, and judicial branches. Additionally, there are questions about the rights and responsibilities of citizens, as well as significant historical events and figures that have shaped the nation.

The test also includes questions related to the Bill of Rights, the Constitution, the Declaration of Independence, and other important founding documents. It ensures applicants have a comprehensive understanding of the principles and values upon which the United States was built.

Study Materials

To help applicants prepare for the 2008 Civics Test, the United States Citizenship and Immigration Services (USCIS) provides study materials. These materials include the official list of 100 questions and answers, study guides, flashcards, and additional resources.

The study materials are readily available on the USCIS website and can be accessed by applicants to familiarize themselves with the content and format of the test. It is crucial for applicants to utilize these materials effectively during their preparation.

Passing Requirements

To pass the 2008 Civics Test, applicants must correctly answer at least six out of ten randomly selected questions. The USCIS officer administering the test will ask the questions orally, and the applicant must provide their answers.

The officer will determine the accuracy of the responses and evaluate whether the applicant has met the passing requirement. It is important for applicants to listen carefully to each question and provide accurate and complete answers to demonstrate their knowledge and understanding.

Importance of the 2008 Civics Test

The 2008 Civics Test is designed to assess applicants' familiarity with the principles, history, and governance of the United States. It holds significant importance in the naturalization process as it ensures that individuals seeking U.S. citizenship have a solid foundation of knowledge about the country they aspire to join.

By demonstrating their understanding of American civics, applicants show their commitment to becoming active and engaged citizens. The test promotes civic education and encourages individuals to be informed about their rights, responsibilities, and the democratic processes that govern the nation.

A comprehensive understanding of American civics empowers new citizens to actively participate in their communities, contribute to the democratic process, and make informed decisions as they exercise their rights and fulfill their responsibilities.

Preparation Strategies

To successfully prepare for the 2008 Civics Test, applicants can employ various strategies:

a. **Study the official materials:** Applicants should thoroughly study the official list of 100 questions and answers from USCIS. They should familiarize themselves with the content and ensure a deep understanding of the principles, historical events, and governance systems covered in the test.

b. **Use study guides and resources:** USCIS provides study guides and supplementary resources to aid in the preparation process. These guides offer explanations, examples, and additional information to enhance applicants' understanding of the test material. Utilizing these resources can help applicants gain a comprehensive grasp of American civics.

c. **Practice with sample tests:** Applicants can benefit from practicing sample tests and answering the questions within a limited time frame. This helps develop time management skills and allows individuals to become more comfortable with the format and structure of the test. Regular practice can also identify areas that require further study and improvement.

d. **Seek support and collaboration:** Joining study groups or partnering with fellow applicants can be beneficial. Collaborative learning allows for discussion, clarification, and sharing of knowledge. Engaging in study sessions with others can enhance understanding, provide different perspectives, and foster a supportive learning environment.

e. **Stay updated:** It is important to stay informed about any updates or changes to the test. USCIS occasionally revises the questions and answers to reflect current events or constitutional amendments. Applicants should regularly check the USCIS website for updates and ensure that their study materials align with the most recent version of the test.

f. **Engage with supplementary resources:** Supplementing study materials with additional resources such as books, documentaries, and educational websites can provide a deeper understanding of American history, government, and civic principles. Exploring these resources can further enhance applicants' knowledge and preparation for the test.

The 2008 Civics Test is a significant component of the naturalization process, evaluating applicants' knowledge of American government, history, and civic principles. By studying the official materials, utilizing study guides, practicing with sample tests, and staying updated, applicants can enhance their chances of success. The test promotes informed citizenship, fosters a sense of belonging, and empowers new citizens to contribute meaningfully to their communities.

2.2.2 The 2020 Version

The Civics Test version 2020, though now applicable in very few cases, remains an important component of the naturalization process in the United States. It is designed to assess the knowledge of applicants of American government, history, and civic principles, ensuring they have a solid understanding of the country they wish to become citizens of. Let's delve into the key aspects of the 2020 Civics Test:

Question Format: The 2020 Civics Test consists of 128 questions. Contrary to previous versions, the questions are not multiple-choice. Instead, they are open response, requiring the applicant to provide their own answers. This format allows the USCIS officer to evaluate the applicant's knowledge across a wide range of topics related to American civics.

Content Coverage:
The questions in the 2020 Civics Test cover various aspects of American government, history, and civic principles. They explore topics such as the principles of American democracy, the governance system, the rights and responsibilities of citizens, and significant historical events. The test aims to ensure that applicants have a comprehensive understanding of the fundamental principles that shape the United States.

Additionally, the 2020 version introduces questions specific to certain historical periods and events. This includes questions about the American Revolution, the Civil Rights Movement, the Civil War, and more recent events in American history. These additions reflect the dynamic nature of the United States and its evolving civic landscape.

Study Materials: The USCIS provides study materials to help applicants prepare for the 2020 Civics Test. These materials include the official list of 128 questions and answers, study guides, flashcards, and other resources. Applicants are encouraged to utilize these materials to familiarize themselves with the content and format of the test.

The study materials are easily accessible on the USCIS website and are available in multiple formats, including digital and printable versions. They provide applicants with the necessary information to acquire a strong foundation in American civics and prepare them for the test effectively.

Passing Requirements: To pass the 2020 Civics Test, applicants must correctly answer at least 12 of 20 questions. The USCIS officer administering the test will ask the questions orally, and the applicant must provide their answers. The officer will assess the accuracy of the responses to determine whether the applicant meets the passing requirement.

It is essential for applicants to listen attentively to each question and respond with accurate and complete answers. Demonstrating a solid grasp of American civics is crucial to passing the test and progressing in the naturalization process.

Importance of the 2020 Civics Test: The 2020 Civics Test plays a vital role in the naturalization process by evaluating an applicant's knowledge of American civics. It ensures that individuals seeking U.S. citizenship are well-informed about the principles, history, and governance of the country. By demonstrating their understanding, applicants show their commitment to becoming engaged and responsible citizens.

The test promotes civic education and encourages applicants to learn about the rights and responsibilities associated with U.S. citizenship. It equips them with the knowledge necessary to actively participate in their communities, make informed decisions, and contribute positively to the democratic processes of the nation.

Choice Between the Two Tests

A limited number of applicants may have the option to undertake the 2020 version of the Civics Test.

If your Form N-400, Application for Naturalization, was filed between December 1, 2020, and March 1, 2021, and your initial examination (interview) was scheduled prior to April 19, 2021, you have the discretion to opt for either the 2008 or 2020 civics test during the naturalization process. All other applicants will be mandated to undertake the 2008 civics test.

To ascertain if you are required to take the 2008 civics test, or if you have the choice between the 2008 and 2020 civics test, please follow these steps:

1. Verify your filing date, also known as a "received date" on your N-400 notice at the top left corner (see sample notice to the right).
2. Once you have your received date, refer to the table below and identify the scenario that applies to you based on your filing and initial examination dates.

My filing date (also known as a received date) for my N-400 is:	My initial examination (interview) is scheduled:	Which test will I take at my initial examination (interview)?	If I fail the civics test, which test will I take at my re-exam?	Which test will I take at my N-336 hearing? *
Before Dec. 1, 2020 (12/1/2020)	on any date	2008 Civics Test	2008 Civics Test	2008 Civics Test
On or after Dec. 1, 2020 (12/1/2020) and before March 1, 2021 (03/01/2021)	before April 19, 2021 (04/19/2021)	You can choose between the 2020 Civics Test or 2008 Civics Test	You can choose between the 2020 Civics Test or 2008 Civics Test	You can choose between the 2020 Civics Test or 2008 Civics Test
On or after Dec. 1, 2020, (12/1/2020) and before March 1, 2021 (03/01/2021)	on or after April 19, 2021 (4/19/2021)	2008 Civics Test	2008 Civics Test	2008 Civics Test
On or after March 1, 2021 (03/01/2021)	on any date	2008 Civics Test	2008 Civics Test	2008 Civics Test

2.3 Full or Partial Exemptions for English Test or Civics Test

When obtaining U.S. citizenship through naturalization, applicants are typically required to demonstrate proficiency in the English language and pass the Civics Test. However, certain individuals may be eligible for full or partial exemptions from these requirements based on specific circumstances. Let's explore the criteria and considerations for full or partial exemptions for the English Test or Civics Test.

2.3.1 English Test Exemptions

The English Test is designed to assess an applicant's ability to speak, understand, read, and write in the English language. While most applicants are required to take and pass this test, there are exemptions available for certain individuals:

-   **Age Exemptions:** Applicants who are 50 years of age or older at the time of filing their naturalization application and have lived in the United States as lawful permanent residents (LPRs) for at least 20 years are eligible for an exemption from the English Test. This exemption, known as the "50/20" exception, recognizes the substantial contribution and longstanding residence of older applicants. Similarly, applicants who are 55 years of age or older at the time of filing their naturalization application and have lived in the United States as LPRs for at least 15 years are also eligible for the same exemption.

- **Medical Disability Exemptions:** Applicants with certain physical or developmental disabilities that prevent them from acquiring or demonstrating the required English language skills may be eligible for a medical disability exemption. To qualify for this exemption, applicants must provide appropriate medical documentation supporting their disability and its impact on their language abilities. USCIS carefully reviews medical evidence to determine eligibility for this exemption.
- **Accommodations for Disabilities:** Even if an applicant does not meet the criteria for a full exemption, USCIS provides accommodations for individuals with disabilities. Applicants with documented disabilities affecting their ability to speak, understand, read, or write in English may request reasonable accommodations during the naturalization process, such as additional time for the English Test or the use of assistive devices.

2.3.2 Civics Test Exemptions

The Civics Test evaluates an applicant's knowledge of the U.S. government, history, and civic principles. While most applicants are required to take and pass this test, there are exemptions available for certain individuals:

a. **Age and Residence Exemptions:** Applicants who are 65 years of age or older and have been living in the United States as LPRs for at least 20 years when filing their naturalization application are eligible for an exemption from the Civics Test. This exemption, known as the "65/20" exception, acknowledges the long-term residence and life experiences of older individuals.

b. **Medical Disability Exemptions:** Like the English Test, applicants with certain physical or developmental disabilities that prevent them from acquiring or demonstrating the required knowledge for the Civics Test may be eligible for a medical disability exemption. Medical documentation supporting the disability and its impact on the applicant's ability to learn or demonstrate knowledge is necessary to qualify for this exemption.

c. **Accommodations for Disabilities:** USCIS provides accommodations for individuals with disabilities who may face challenges in taking the Civics Test. Applicants with documented disabilities that affect their ability to learn or demonstrate knowledge may request reasonable accommodations, such as modified test formats, auxiliary aids, or additional time.

2.3.3 Partial Exemptions

In some cases, applicants may be eligible for partial exemptions, which means they must fulfill certain requirements but with modified criteria. These exemptions acknowledge that individuals may face challenges in meeting all the standard requirements due to age, medical conditions, or disabilities:

a. **Reduced English Test:** Applicants who qualify for the "50/20" or "55/15" age exemptions are still required to demonstrate a basic understanding of the English language and must complete a simplified version of the English Test. The simplified test consists of a shorter vocabulary list and fewer reading and writing questions.

b. Reduced Civics Test: Similarly, applicants who meet the "65/20" age exemption are still required to demonstrate a basic understanding of the U.S. government and history but with a modified version of the Civics Test. The modified test consists of 20 questions instead of the standard 100 questions. Applicants must answer 10 out of the 20 questions correctly to pass the test.

2.3.4 Documentation and Process

To be considered for full or partial exemptions, applicants must provide appropriate documentation and evidence to support their eligibility. This may include medical records, official documents confirming age and residency, or disability-related documentation from qualified professionals.

It is important for applicants to carefully review the USCIS guidelines and requirements regarding exemptions and accommodations. They should consult official USCIS resources, such as the USCIS website, or seek guidance from immigration professionals to ensure they have the most up-to-date and accurate information regarding eligibility criteria, documentation requirements, and the process to request exemptions or accommodations.

Full or partial exemptions for the English Test or Civics Test provide opportunities for individuals who face challenges due to age, medical conditions, or disabilities to pursue naturalization. These exemptions acknowledge the unique circumstances of certain applicants while still maintaining the importance of English language proficiency and civic knowledge for the naturalization process. By understanding the eligibility criteria and following the proper procedures for requesting exemptions or accommodations, individuals can navigate the naturalization process more effectively and work towards achieving their goal of becoming U.S. citizens.

Remember, it is essential to consult official USCIS resources and seek professional advice to ensure compliance with current guidelines and requirements. USCIS reserves the right to update its policies and procedures, so staying informed is crucial throughout the naturalization process.

Chapter 3: The English Language Test

The English Language Test is vital to the naturalization process in the United States. It evaluates an applicant's ability to communicate effectively in English, which is essential for daily life, civic engagement, and participation in American society. The test consists of three main sections: the Spoken Language Exam, the Reading Test, and the Writing Exam. Each section assesses different aspects of English language proficiency and aims to ensure applicants have the necessary language skills to become U.S. citizens.

3.1 Spoken Language Exam

The Spoken Language Exam is a vital component of the English Language Test in the naturalization process. It aims to assess an applicant's ability to understand and respond to spoken English, as well as their overall oral communication skills. During the exam, a USCIS officer asks questions based on the information provided in the N400 form, which is the Application for Naturalization. These questions evaluate the applicant's comprehension, vocabulary, pronunciation, and ability to express themselves clearly in English.

Understanding the N400 Model

Before we delve into the examples of N400-based questions, it is crucial to understand the basic principles of the N400 model.

By using N400-based questions in the spoken language exam, examiners can gauge a candidate's ability to comprehend the meaning and make semantic connections within a given context. These questions assess the candidate's vocabulary, understanding of sentence structure, and overall language proficiency.

Types of Questions

The questions asked during the Spoken Language Exam cover various topics to ensure that applicants can communicate effectively in different situations. Here are some examples of the types of questions that may be asked on the N400 Model:

Personal Information:

- What is your full name?
- When and where were you born?
- What is your current address?
- How long have you been living there?

These questions verify the applicant's personal details and help establish their identity and residency. They are relatively straightforward and allow the applicant to provide concise answers based on their information.

Family and Marital Status:

- Are you married? If yes, what is your spouse's name and date of birth?
- Do you have any children? If yes, what are their names and ages?

These questions aim to gather information about the applicant's family and marital status. They help establish family ties and relationships, which can be important for immigration and citizenship purposes.

Employment and Education:

- What is your current occupation?
- Where do you work, and how long have you been employed there?
- Have you attended any schools or universities in the United States?

These questions focus on the applicant's employment and educational background. They provide insights into the applicant's work history, professional skills, and educational qualifications.

Travel and Residence:

- Have you traveled outside the United States in the past five years? If yes, where did you go and when?
- How long have you been a lawful permanent resident in the United States?

These questions explore the applicant's travel history and residency status. They help establish the applicant's presence in the United States and ensure compliance with immigration laws.

Moral Character:

- Have you ever been arrested or convicted of a crime? If yes, please provide details.

This question addresses the applicant's moral character and requires them to disclose any criminal history. It is crucial for determining eligibility for naturalization and assessing an applicant's adherence to the legal and ethical standards of U.S. citizenship.

3.1.1 Examples of N400-Based Questions

Now let us explore some examples of N400-based questions that may be included in the spoken language exam. These questions are designed to challenge the candidate's language skills and their ability to interpret meaning effectively.

Example 1

- Examiner: "Can you describe your favorite childhood memory?"
- N400-based question: "What emotions were you experiencing during that particular memory?"

In this example, the candidate is expected to recall a specific childhood memory and describe the associated emotions. The N400-based question requires the candidate to tap into their semantic knowledge and understand the relationship between memory and emotions. A comprehensive answer would demonstrate the candidate's ability to express emotions accurately and provide relevant details about the memory.

Example 2

- Examiner: "What do you think are the advantages and disadvantages of social media?"
- N400-based question: "How do you think social media has influenced interpersonal relationships?"

This question challenges the candidate to consider the impact of social media on interpersonal relationships. By asking about the influence of social media, the N400-based question aims to assess the candidate's ability to understand the broader implications of a societal phenomenon. A well-structured response would demonstrate critical thinking skills, an understanding of social dynamics, and the ability to provide examples or evidence to support their viewpoint.

Example 3

- Examiner: "Describe a time when you had to resolve a conflict with a coworker."
- N400-based question: "What strategies did you use to reach a resolution, and what were the outcomes?"

This N400-based question requires candidates to reflect on a specific situation and describe their problem-solving skills and conflict-resolution strategies. It assesses their ability to understand the nuances of a workplace conflict and their proficiency in expressing their actions and the resulting outcomes. A comprehensive answer would demonstrate effective communication skills, empathy, and the ability to navigate challenging interpersonal situations.

It is important for applicants to prepare for the Spoken Language Exam by practicing their English-speaking skills. Engaging in conversations with native English speakers, participating in language exchange programs, and working with a language tutor can help applicants improve their oral communication abilities and feel more confident during the exam.

Applicants should strive to develop a solid command of vocabulary and grammar, and work on their pronunciation and intonation. Regular practice listening and responding to questions in English will enhance their ability to understand spoken English and provide clear and concise answers. Additionally, applicants can utilize resources such as language learning apps, online courses, and language study materials to further improve their language skills.

Preparing for the Spoken Language Exam helps applicants pass the naturalization process and equips them with the necessary English language skills to engage in everyday conversations, communicate effectively in the workplace, and actively participate in American society. Mastering spoken English is essential for immigrants seeking to integrate into their new communities, build relationships, and fully embrace the opportunities that come with U.S. citizenship.

3.2 Reading Test

The Reading Test evaluates an applicant's ability to understand written English, including basic sentences and passages. The purpose of this test is to ensure that applicants can read and comprehend information necessary for daily life as well as fully participate in American society.

During the Reading Test, applicants are presented with several sentences that they must read aloud to demonstrate their reading proficiency. These sentences are carefully chosen to cover a range of vocabulary, grammar structures, and sentence types. The USCIS officer administering the test evaluates the applicant's pronunciation, word recognition, and comprehension skills.

Understanding the Reading Test

The reading test evaluates a candidate's reading comprehension skills, vocabulary, and overall understanding of written English. It typically consists of a series of passages or sentences followed by questions that assess the candidate's ability to extract information, infer meaning, and make connections within the text.

The USCIS reading vocabulary list is a valuable resource for candidates preparing for the English Language Test. It contains a compilation of words frequently used in USCIS reading materials, which include topics related to American history, government, and civics. By studying this vocabulary list, candidates can enhance their reading skills and familiarize themselves with the terminology commonly found in the reading test.

Types of Sentences

To give you an idea of the types of sentences that may be included in the Reading Test, here are some examples:

Simple Sentences:
- "The cat is on the mat."
- "I have a blue pen."
- "She is reading a book."

These simple sentences contain common words and straightforward grammar. They test the applicant's ability to read and pronounce words accurately, as well as their ability to understand basic sentence structures.

Questions and Responses:
- Question: "What is your name?" Response: "My name is John."
- Question: "Where do you live?" Response: "I live in New York."

These sentences assess the applicant's ability to read and understand questions and respond appropriately. They also test the applicant's comprehension of common question words and their ability to provide relevant answers.

Instructions:
- "Please sign your name here."
- "Read the sentence and then answer the question."

These sentences evaluate the applicant's comprehension of written instructions. They assess the applicant's ability to follow directions and understand what is expected of them.

Descriptions:
- "The weather today is sunny and warm."
- "The car is red and has four doors."

These sentences require the applicant to read and comprehend descriptive information. They test the applicant's ability to understand and interpret details about people, objects, or situations.

Short Passages:
- "Mary went to the store to buy some milk and bread."
- "John likes to play soccer with his friends in the park."

These sentences present short passages that require the applicant to read and understand a short narrative. They assess the applicant's ability to extract meaning from context and comprehend a cohesive text.

3.2.1 Examples of Sentences from the USCIS Reading Vocabulary List

Let us explore some examples of sentences that incorporate words extracted from the USCIS reading vocabulary list. These examples will illustrate the types of sentences candidates may encounter in the reading test and demonstrate how to approach them effectively.

Example 1

- Sentence: "The Declaration of Independence, a fundamental document in American history, was adopted on July 4, 1776."

In this sentence, the candidate must read and understand the sentence in its entirety, paying attention to important details such as the significance of the Declaration of Independence and the date it was adopted. The words "Declaration of Independence" and "adopted" are directly related to American history and are part of the USCIS reading vocabulary list. A correct reading of this sentence would demonstrate the candidate's ability to comprehend historical events and their understanding of key terms.

Example 2

- Sentence: "The United States Constitution establishes the framework for the federal government and outlines the rights and freedoms of its citizens."

This sentence tests the candidate's comprehension of the United States Constitution and its significance. Key words such as "Constitution," "establish," "framework," "federal government," "rights," and "freedoms" are all part of the USCIS reading vocabulary list. A correct reading of this sentence would indicate the candidate's understanding of the Constitution's role in governing the United States and their grasp of key constitutional terms.

Example 3

- Sentence: "The Great Depression, a severe economic downturn in the 1930s, had a profound impact on the lives of many Americans."

This sentence challenges the candidate's ability to comprehend historical events and their consequences. The words "Great Depression," "economic downturn," "1930s," and "impact" are all relevant terms from the USCIS reading vocabulary list. A correct reading of this sentence would demonstrate the candidate's knowledge of major historical events and their understanding of the far-reaching effects of the Great Depression.

Approaching the Reading Test

To excel in the reading test, candidates should employ effective reading strategies and develop a strong vocabulary. Here are some tips to enhance performance in the reading test:

1. **Build vocabulary:** Familiarize yourself with words from the USCIS reading vocabulary list and practice using them in sentences. Read widely on various topics to expand your vocabulary and improve your ability to comprehend different types of texts.
2. **Actively read:** Read the sentence or passage carefully, paying attention to key details, main ideas, and any supporting information provided. Underline or highlight important words or phrases that may help you answer the accompanying questions accurately.
3. **Look for context clues:** Use context clues to understand the meaning of unfamiliar words. Look for surrounding words or phrases that can provide hints about the word's definition or usage within the sentence.
4. **Practice skimming and scanning:** Develop the ability to quickly skim through a passage to get a general understanding of the content. Then, scan the passage for specific information required to answer the questions.
5. **Answer strategically:** Read the questions carefully and refer back to the passage to find the relevant information needed to answer each question. Avoid making assumptions or relying solely on prior knowledge.

It is crucial for applicants to prepare for the Reading Test by practicing their reading skills in English. Regular reading of English texts, such as books, newspapers, magazines, and online articles, can help applicants improve their vocabulary, comprehension, and reading speed. Additionally, using English language learning resources focusing on reading comprehension exercises and strategies can be beneficial.

Applicants should pay attention to pronunciation and intonation when reading the sentences during the test. Clear and accurate pronunciation is essential for effective communication, and it demonstrates the applicant's ability to convey meaning through spoken English.

To enhance their reading skills, applicants can also employ strategies such as skimming and scanning, which involve quickly looking through a text for specific information or a general understanding. These techniques can be valuable during the test to locate relevant details and answer questions accurately.

Practicing reading aloud and discussing the content of various texts with a language partner or tutor can also be helpful. Engaging in conversations about the text allows applicants to improve their comprehension, expand their vocabulary, and develop their ability to express their thoughts and opinions in English.

The Reading Test not only assesses an applicant's reading skills but also allows them to further improve their English language proficiency. The ability to read and understand written English is essential for accessing information, engaging with written materials, and participating fully in educational, professional, and social contexts as a citizen of the United States.

Applicants who dedicate time and effort to strengthening their reading skills will perform well in the Reading Test and develop the language abilities necessary for success and integration in their new home country.

3.3 Writing Exam

The Writing Exam assesses an applicant's ability to communicate in written English, including grammar, vocabulary, sentence structure, and coherence. The purpose of this exam is to ensure that applicants can effectively convey their thoughts and ideas in writing, as written communication is crucial for various aspects of daily life, such as filling out forms, writing emails, and participating in educational and professional settings.

During the Writing Exam, applicants are presented with prompts or questions that require them to write short responses or complete sentences. The USCIS officer evaluates the applicant's writing skills based on various criteria, including grammar, spelling, punctuation, vocabulary usage, sentence structure, and overall clarity of expression.

The Importance of the Writing Exam

The writing exam is a crucial part of the English Language Test as it evaluates a candidate's proficiency in written English, including grammar, vocabulary, sentence structure, and coherence. Effective writing skills are essential for various purposes, such as academic studies, professional communication, and everyday written interactions. The writing exam aims to assess a candidate's ability to convey their thoughts accurately and coherently in written form.

Types of Tasks

To provide an understanding of the types of writing tasks and examples of correctly written sentences that may be included in the Writing Exam, let's explore some common scenarios:

Completing Sentences

Applicants may be asked to complete a sentence by filling in the missing word or phrase. For example:

- "My favorite color is _____."
- Correct response: "blue."
- "I have two _____."
- Correct response: "brothers."

In these cases, applicants need to demonstrate their understanding of sentence structure and appropriate word choice. The correct response should fit grammatically and contextually within the given sentence.

Short Responses

Applicants may be asked to provide brief answers or responses to specific prompts. For example:

- "What is your favorite hobby?" Correct response: "I enjoy playing the piano in my free time."
- "Describe your ideal vacation destination." Correct response: "My ideal vacation destination would be a tropical island with beautiful beaches and clear blue waters."

These prompts assess the applicant's ability to convey relevant information in a coherent and concise manner. The responses should demonstrate appropriate vocabulary usage, sentence structure, and clarity of expression.

Writing a Simple Sentence

Applicants may be asked to write a simple sentence based on a given prompt or picture. For example:

- Prompt: "Write a sentence about your family." Correct response: "I have a loving and supportive family who always encourages me."

This type of task evaluates the applicant's ability to construct grammatically correct sentences and express ideas accurately.

Descriptive Writing

Applicants may be asked to describe a person, place, or object based on a provided prompt or picture. For example:

- Prompt: "Describe your favorite childhood memory." Correct response: "One of my favorite childhood memories is playing hide-and-seek with my friends in the neighborhood park. We would spend hours laughing and having fun."

Descriptive writing tasks test the applicant's ability to use appropriate adjectives, adverbs, and descriptive language to vividly communicate their experiences or impressions.

Responding to a Scenario

Applicants may be given a scenario or situation and asked to write a response or express an opinion. For example:

- Scenario: "You witnessed a random act of kindness. Write about what you saw and how it made you feel." Correct response: "I recently saw a stranger help an elderly person carry their groceries to their car. It was heartwarming to witness such kindness, and reminded me of the importance of compassion and empathy in our society."

These types of prompts evaluate the applicant's ability to express their thoughts, opinions, and emotions effectively in writing.

Examples of Writing Exam Format

Let us explore some examples of the writing exam format that allows three attempts to write a correct sentence in English. These examples will illustrate the types of sentences candidates may be asked to write and demonstrate how to approach them effectively.

Example 1:

- Prompt: Write a sentence using the word "appreciate."
- Attempt 1: I appreciate my parents.
- Feedback: The sentence is grammatically correct but lacks context or additional details. Try to provide more information or examples to make the sentence more complete and meaningful.
- Attempt 2: I appreciate my parents for their unwavering support and love throughout my life.
- Feedback: Great improvement! The sentence now includes additional information that adds depth and meaning. However, consider using more specific examples or details to further enhance the sentence.

- Attempt 3: I genuinely appreciate my parents for their unwavering support and love, which they have shown me through their guidance, sacrifices, and encouragement in every aspect of my life.
- Feedback: Excellent! The third attempt provides a well-rounded and comprehensive sentence. It expresses appreciation and highlights specific actions and qualities of the parents, making the sentence more engaging and meaningful.

Example 2:
- Prompt: Write a sentence using the word "consequence."
- Attempt 1: The consequence was bad.
- Feedback: While the sentence is grammatically correct, it lacks specificity and fails to provide sufficient context. Try to elaborate on the consequence and its impact to make the sentence more informative and engaging.
- Attempt 2: The consequence of the decision was negative and had far-reaching effects on the entire organization.
- Feedback: Good improvement! The second attempt introduces the idea of a decision and its consequence. However, consider providing more specific details about the decision and its effects to make the sentence more descriptive and impactful.
- Attempt 3: The ill-informed decision to cut corners in the manufacturing process had severe consequences, leading to a significant decline in product quality and customer satisfaction.
- Feedback: Well done! The third attempt provides a detailed and concise sentence that effectively demonstrates the consequences of the decision. It offers specific information about the decision, the resulting impact, and the implications for product quality and customer satisfaction.

Example 3:
- Prompt: Write a sentence using the word "accomplish."
- Attempt 1: I want to accomplish my goals.
- Feedback: The sentence is grammatically correct but lacks specificity. Try to provide more details about the goals or the actions required to accomplish them.
- Attempt 2: I am determined to accomplish my long-term goals through consistent hard work, perseverance, and continuous self-improvement.
- Feedback: Good improvement! The second attempt introduces the concept of long-term goals and the qualities needed to achieve them. However, consider adding more specific examples or details to make the sentence more vivid and engaging.
- Attempt 3: By setting clear objectives, developing a strategic plan, and embracing challenges with resilience, I will accomplish my long-term goals and transform my vision into reality.
- Feedback: Excellent! The third attempt provides a comprehensive sentence that not only expresses the intention to accomplish goals but also highlights the necessary actions and mindset required. It demonstrates a strong sense of determination and a clear understanding of the steps needed to achieve success.

Approaching the Writing Exam

To excel in the writing exam, candidates should adopt effective writing strategies and develop strong writing skills. Here are some tips to enhance performance in the writing exam:

1. **Understand the Prompt:** Read the prompt carefully and ensure a clear understanding of what is being asked. Identify important words or concepts and consider any specific instructions provided.

2. **Plan and Organize:** Before writing, take a few minutes to brainstorm ideas and outline your response. Organize your thoughts, identify important points, and determine the logical flow of your sentence or paragraph.
3. **Use Correct Grammar and Vocabulary:** Pay attention to grammar, punctuation, and spelling. Use appropriate vocabulary and sentence structures to convey your ideas accurately.
4. **Provide Context and Details:** Whenever possible, provide context, examples, or supporting details to enrich your sentences. This enhances clarity and engages the reader.
5. **Revise and Edit:** Leave time at the end to revise and edit your writing. Check for errors, clarity, coherence, and overall effectiveness of your sentence or paragraph.

During the Writing Exam, it is crucial for applicants to pay attention to grammar, spelling, punctuation, and sentence structure. Clear and concise writing that effectively conveys the intended message is essential for successful communication.

To improve their writing skills and prepare for the Writing Exam, applicants can practice various writing exercises, such as journaling, writing short paragraphs or essays, and seeking feedback from English language tutors or native speakers. Additionally, utilizing grammar and writing resources, such as grammar guides and vocabulary books, can help applicants strengthen their language skills and become more confident writers.

It is important to note that the Writing Exam is not about producing lengthy or complex compositions. Instead, it focuses on the applicant's ability to communicate effectively in written English using correct grammar, vocabulary, and sentence structure. Applicants should strive to express their thoughts clearly and concisely while adhering to the given prompts.

By dedicating time and effort to improving their writing skills, applicants can enhance their overall English language proficiency and increase their chances of success in the naturalization process. Effective written communication skills will assist them during the exam and empower them to participate actively in educational, professional, and social contexts as proud citizens of the United States.

Chapter 4: The Civic Education Test

4.1 The 2008 Test: The Importance of Updating Some Answers Based on the Elections

According to a notice published in the Federal Register, the Department of Homeland Security (DHS) intends to conduct a trial test of proposed changes to the current naturalization test. The trial test will involve volunteers from community-based organizations. U.S. Citizenship and Immigration Services (USCIS) has scheduled a virtual engagement on May 31, 2023, to offer a comprehensive presentation on the proposed changes and the trial test. If you have any comments regarding the pilot test, you can submit them to natzredesign22@uscis.dhs.gov. Further updates and information will be posted on the Citizenship Resource Center page as they become available.

On the Civics Test, some answers may be subject to change due to federal or state elections, certain judicial appointments, or changes or updates in the law. You will be required to answer the question with the name of the official in office at the time of your naturalization interview. On this page, you will find the answers that may have changed on the citizenship test for the 2008 version of the test.

If you are 65 years of age or older and have been a lawful permanent resident of the United States for 20 years or more, you have the option to focus your study efforts solely on the questions marked with an asterisk (*) at the end of each question. Please note that the U.S. government websites listed below may not have the most up-to-date information. USCIS does not assume responsibility for maintaining or updating these sites. To obtain the names of your elected state officials, please refer to your official state government website.

A: American Democracy Principles

1. What is the supreme law of the land?

Right answer: The Constitution

Explanation: In 1787, the United States' Founding Fathers created the Constitution. The United States Constitution is considered the "supreme law of the land." The Constitution of the United States of America has stood the test of time better than the constitutions of any other nation. It lays forth the fundamental ideas upon which the government of the United States is based. The type of governance that is established by the Constitution is referred to as "representative democracy." In a kind of democracy known as representative democracy, voters vote for those who will represent them in legislative bodies. In addition, residents of the United States vote for a president to serve as the head of the executive branch of government. The Constitution lays forth the essential rights that are guaranteed to all persons residing in the United States, regardless of citizenship status. The Constitution of the United States must always be followed when writing new laws.

2. What does the Constitution do?

Correct answers (choose one):

- Defines the government
- Protects basic rights of Americans
- Sets up the government

Explanation: The Constitution of the United States of America establishes a system that subdivides governmental authority between the federal government and the state governments. The term "federalism" refers to this system of power distribution. The concept of federalism plays a significant role in the Constitution. We refer to the men who authored the Constitution as the "Framers" of the Constitution. These men were the Founding Fathers. To achieve their goal of reducing the scope of the federal government's authority, the Founding Fathers divided its functions into three distinct branches: the executive, the legislative, and the judiciary. The Constitution details the authority vested in each of the three branches of government. The term "amendments" refers to the alterations and additions that have been made to the Constitution. The name "Bill of Rights" refers to the first ten amendments of the Constitution. The Bill of Rights outlined the rights and freedoms that are guaranteed to each American citizen.

3. The idea of self-government is in the first three words of the Constitution. What are these words?

Correct answer: We the People

Explanation: According to the Constitution, "We the People of the United States, in Order to form a more perfect Union, establish Justice, insure domestic Tranquility, provide for the common defense, promote the general Welfare, and secure the Blessings of Liberty to ourselves and our Posterity, do ordain and establish this Constitution for the United States of America." In the Constitution, it is stated that "We the People" are the ones who are responsible for establishing the government. The people are the government's primary concern, and it strives to preserve their rights. The people of the United States are the ones who have the most authority, and as such, they are the ones who hold the power to rule. This concept is referred to as "popular sovereignty." The laws are created via the people's elected representatives.

4. What is an amendment?
Correct answers (choose one):
- A change (to the Constitution) or
- An addition (to the Constitution)

Explanation: A modification or addition to the Constitution is referred to as an amendment. The Founding Fathers of the United States were aware that a nation's laws are subject to modification as time passes. They did not want to make it too simple to change the Constitution, which is the highest law in the nation, so that was a concern. Additionally, the Founding Fathers did not want the Constitution stripped of its original intent. Because of this, they concluded that there were only two ways the United States Congress could make constitutional amendments: by a vote of two-thirds in both the Senate and the House of Representatives, or by calling a special convention. Two-thirds of the states are required to put in a request for an extraordinary convention. After an amendment has been approved by Congress or by a special convention, it must next be ratified (accepted) by the legislatures of three-fourths of the states in order for the amendment to become law. Another method for ratifying the amendment is to hold a special convention in three-quarters of the states. Some of the suggested adjustments will not be accepted. There have been six occasions in the history of the United States when amendments were voted on by Congress but not adopted by enough states to be ratified.

5. What do we call the first ten amendments to the Constitution?
Right answer: The Bill of Rights

Explanation: The first 10 amendments to the Constitution are collectively called the Bill of Rights. Individual rights were not a primary concern for the Founding Fathers when they drafted the Constitution. Their primary emphasis was on putting together the framework for the new government. Many individuals who lived in the United States felt that the Constitution should be used to protect the rights of the people, and they wanted a list of everything that the government was forbidden to do. They were concerned that a strong government would strip citizens of the liberties they had fought for and earned in the Revolutionary War. James Madison, who helped write the Constitution, was responsible for compiling a list of individual rights and limitations on the powers of the government. These rights are outlined in the first ten amendments, which are together referred to as the Bill of Rights. Some of these rights include the freedom of expression, the right to bear arms, the freedom from search without a warrant, the freedom not to be tried twice for the same crime, the right not to testify against yourself in your own trial, the right to a trial by a jury of your peers, the right to an attorney, and protection against excessive fines and unusual punishments. In 1791, the Bill of Rights was officially ratified.

6. What is one right or freedom from the First Amendment?
Correct answers (choose one):
- Speech
- Religion
- Assembly
- Press
- Petition the government

Explanation: The ability of an individual to freely express themselves is safeguarded by the First Amendment of the Bill of Rights. The freedom to express oneself enables open discourse and debate on matters of public concern. It is essential to democracy to have free and open discourse and debate. Both the freedom of religion and the freedom of expression are safeguarded under the First Amendment. According to the provisions of this amendment, the United States Congress is prohibited from passing legislation that constitute a state religion or that impose restrictions on religious expression. Congress cannot make legislation that restricts the freedom of the press or the right of people to freely assemble. People also have the right, according to the First Amendment, to petition the government to modify unjust laws or deeds. This freedom is guaranteed to them. It's possible that Congress won't take away these liberties. These rights are guaranteed and protected by the First Amendment of the Constitution of the United States.

7. What is the total number of amendments present in the Constitution?
Right answer: 27

Explanation: The first 10 amendments were included in the Constitution in 1791. Since then, an additional 17 modifications have been introduced to the document. As of now, there have been 27 amendments added to the Constitution. 1992 saw the ratification of the 27th Amendment. It details the compensation received by senators and representatives. It's interesting to note that the first time this amendment was addressed in Congress was back in 1789 when it was one of the initial amendments being considered for the Bill of Rights.

8. What did the Declaration of Independence do?
Correct answers (choose one):
- Proclaimed our independence from Great Britain
- Expressed our declaration of independence from Great Britain
- Stated that the U.S. has achieved freedom from Great Britain

Explanation: The concepts presented in the Declaration of Independence about the structure of the government in the United States are significant. In the Declaration of Independence, it is stated that "certain unalienable rights" belong to each person since they were born equal. These rights cannot be changed or taken away by the government in any manner. Thomas Jefferson, who penned the Declaration of Independence, argued in it that the thirteen American colonies ought to be free from British rule since the British government did not protect the fundamental rights of the colonists. Jefferson believed a government should only be in place if the people wanted it to be. He was a firm believer in the concept that a nation's citizens should be the ones who establish its government and should provide their consent (or agreement) to abide by the laws that it passes. The phrase "consent of the governed" describes this concept. People will be more willing to comply with laws that have been established by the government if such laws are seen to be just and protective of their rights. Jefferson compiled a list of grievances that the colonies had against the King of England and included it in the Declaration of Independence. The last declaration made by Jefferson in the Declaration was that the colonies already were and ought to continue to exist as free and independent states. On July 4, 1776, a vote was held in the Second Continental Congress to adopt the Declaration of Independence.

9. Which two rights are mentioned in the Declaration of Independence?
Correct answers (choose two):
- Life
- Liberty
- Pursuit of happiness

Explanation: The Founding Fathers included in the Declaration of Independence a list of three rights that they deemed "natural" and "unalienable." They are the right to life, the right to liberty, and the right to seek happiness in one's own way. These served as the inspiration for the founding of the United States of America. Thomas Jefferson and the other Founding Fathers held the belief that all individuals are born with inherent rights that cannot be taken away by the government. These rights are why the government was established in the first place. Because individuals freely cede some of their authority to a governing body, they retain the ability to reclaim that power. As a result of the British government's failure to preserve the colonists' rights, the colonies retook control of their governments and declared their independence from Great Britain.

10. What is freedom of religion?

Right answer: You can practice any religion or not practice a religion.

Explanation: Many diverse factors led people to leave their homelands and settle in what is now the United States, including Spain, France, Holland, England, and others. One of the reasons was because of the freedom of religion. The leaders of several of these nations mandated that their populations must worship in a certain manner and attend a particular place of worship. Some of the subjects desired to establish their own churches because they had religious ideas that differed from those of their rulers. The Pilgrims were the first people to go to what is now the United States of America in search of religious freedom in 1620. The Founding Fathers placed a high value on the right to freely practice any religion. Because of this, the right to freely practice whatever religion one chooses was included in the Constitution as a component of the Bill of Rights. The right to freely practice one's religion is protected by the First Amendment of the Constitution. The phrase "Congress shall make no law respecting an establishment of religion, or prohibiting the free exercise thereof" may be found in the First Amendment of the United States Constitution. The United States Congress is forbidden by the First Amendment from establishing a national religion, and people are guaranteed the freedom to believe in whatever religious tradition they want, or none.

11. What is the economic system in the United States?
Correct answers (choose one):
- Capitalist economy
- Market economy

Explanation: Capitalism is the dominant form of economic organization in the United States. Most companies in the economy of the United States are privately held. Businesses are motivated by both competition and profit. In the marketplace, businesses and customers engage with one another, and pricing is up for negotiation. A "market economy" describes this kind of setup. Businesses are the ones that select what to create, how much of it to produce, and what prices to set in a market economy. Consumers are the ones who determine what they will purchase, when they will buy it, and where they will buy it. Competition, supply, and demand all play a role in determining how firms and consumers choose to spend their money in a market economy.

12. What is the "rule of law"?
Correct answers (choose one):
- Everyone must follow the law
- Leaders must obey the law
- Government must obey the law
- No one is above the law

Explanation: In addition to being a Founding Father, John Adams served as the second President of the United States of America. In his writing, he described our nation as having "a government of laws, and not of men." No individual or organization is above the law. The concept of the rule of law stipulates that everyone, including people and leaders, is required to abide by the laws. In the United States of America, the Constitution of the United States serves as the cornerstone upon which the legal system is built. The United States of America is what's known as a "constitutional democracy," which simply means it's a democracy that also has a constitution. People are inclined to respect the laws in constitutional democracies because such laws are created by the people via their elected representatives. This gives individuals a sense of ownership over the legal system. When all individuals are subject to the same laws, the unique and personal freedoms and rights of each person are better preserved. The rule of law is a concept that serves to ensure that the government safeguards the rights of all its citizens and does not discriminate against any particular group.

B: System of Government

13. Name one branch or part of the government.

Correct answers (choose one):

- Congress
- Legislative
- President
- Executive
- The courts
- Judicial

Explanation: The legislative, executive, and judicial departments of government are all outlined in the Constitution as separate entities. The legislative branch was first established by Article I of the Constitution. In Article I, it is stated that laws are made by Congress. The legislative power in the United States of America resides in Congress, which is comprised of the Senate and the House of Representatives. The executive branch of government is outlined in Article II of the Constitution. The laws that are passed by Congress are carried out by the executive branch. The executive branch is responsible for ensuring that the laws of the United States are followed by everyone. The president is the most senior official in the executive branch of government. In addition to the president and the members of his cabinet, the vice president and other cabinet members make up part of the executive branch. The judicial system is laid forth in the Constitution's Article III, which established the branch. Within the legal system, the Supreme Court has supreme judicial authority. The judicial arm of the government is responsible for determining whether laws and acts taken by the government adhere to the Constitution. This is a very significant obligation that must be met.

14. What prevents any single branch of government from acquiring excessive power?

Correct answers (choose one):

- Checks and balances
- Separation of powers

Explanation: To prevent any one person or organization from amassing an excessive amount of authority, the Constitution divides the power of the government into three distinct branches. A system of checks and balances is established when the government is divided into its three distinct parts. This indicates that each branch can obstruct, or at the very least threaten to obstruct, the operations of the other branches. Here are several examples: A treaty signed by the president but not ratified by the Senate, which is part of the legislative branch, is subject to veto power. This illustrates the legislative branch "checking" the executive branch. It is possible for the United States Supreme Court, which is part of the judicial branch, to overturn a statute that was approved by Congress, which is part of the legislative branch. This illustrates the judicial branch "checking" the legislative branch. The government's authority is restricted because of the separation of powers, which also prohibits the government from infringing upon the rights of the people.

15. Who holds the authority in the executive branch?

Right answer: The President

Explanation: It is the responsibility of the executive branch to carry out, often referred to as execute, federal laws and to enforce laws that Congress has established. The President oversees the Executive Branch of the government. The President of the United States has both the position of Head of State and Head of Government. In addition to other responsibilities, the President of the United States is responsible for selecting ambassadors to represent the United States in other parts of the globe and signing treaties with other nations. The president is also responsible for formulating national policy and making legislative proposals to Congress. The President of the United States selects the heads of several federal departments. A new member of the Supreme Court is appointed by the president whenever there is an open seat on the court. On the other hand, the Senate is in a position to overturn the president's decisions. A good illustration of checks and balances is the limitation placed on the president's authority by this provision.

16. Who makes federal laws?

Correct answers (choose one):

- Congress
- Senate and House of Representatives
- U.S. or national legislature

Explanation: The United States' legal system is mostly shaped by the Congress. In general, a federal law is one that every state and every individual in the United States must comply with. A bill to solve a problem may be proposed by either the Senate or the House of Representatives, depending on which chamber of Congress is in control. When a measure is proposed in the Senate, it is immediately referred to one of the Senate committees. A committee in the Senate is looking at the problem and the measure. When a bill is proposed in the House of Representatives, it is submitted to one of the committees of the House of Representatives for further consideration. After researching the bill, the committee may recommend modifying it in some way. After that, the measure is brought to the whole House or Senate for further deliberation. After each house has passed its own version of the bill, the legislation is often sent to a "conference committee" for further discussion. the House of Representatives and the Senate are represented on the conference committee. This committee deliberates over the measure, works to reconcile the many points of contention, and compiles a report that contains the amended version of the law. The committee will then submit the finalized version of the measure to both chambers of the legislature for approval. The measure is term"d "enrol"ed" if it has received approval from both chambers. When a measure has been registered, the next step is for the president to sign it into law. If the president chooses to sign the measure, it will then be considered a law of the United States.

17. What are the two components that make up the U.S. Congress?

Right answer: The Senate and House of Representatives

Explanation: The Senate and the House of Representatives each have their distinct functions inside Congress. The United States Congress is said to be "bicameral" because it is composed of two separate "chambers." In Congress, there is a functioning system of checks and balances. Each of these chambers has its own unique set of responsibilities and abilities. For instance, the Senate is the only body that has the authority to veto a treaty that has been signed by the president or a person whom the president has chosen to serve on the Supreme Court. It is only possible for a measure to be introduced in the House of Representatives that would mandate tax payments from American citizens.

18. What is the total number of U.S. senators?

Right answer: 100

Explanation: There are 100 senators in Congress, with two senators representing each state. Because each state has the same number of senators, there is a level playing field in the Senate between all of the states. There is no difference in the number of senators between states with very big populations and ones with extremely low populations. Those who wrote the Constitution set several provisions to ensure that the Senate would have a limited membership. Because of this, it would be easier to maintain order than in the more chaotic House of Representatives. In *Federalist Paper #63,* James Madison argued that the Senate ought to be a "temperate and respectable body of citizens" that does its business in a "cool and deliberate" manner.

19. For how many years does a U.S. senator serve?

Right answer: 6

Explanation: The Founding Fathers intended for senators to remain free from the influence of popular sentiment when they drafted the Constitution. They believed that a term that was reasonably lengthy and would last for six years would provide them with this protection. They also wanted Senate terms to be longer to counteract the shorter two-year terms of members of the House, who would be more responsive to changes in public opinion because of their shorter tenure. The number of terms a senator may serve is not restricted in any way by the Constitution. Even-numbered years are reserved for holding elections for senators in the United States. At the end of every even-numbered year, one-third of the seats in the Senate are up for election.

20. Who currently represents your state as one of its U.S. Senators?

Right answer: The answer will vary based on where the applicant lives. Note: District of Columbia residents and those living in U.S. territories should answer that D.C. (or the territory where they live) has no senators.

21. The House of Representatives has how many voting members?

Right answer: 435

Explanation: The House of Representatives is the more populous and influential of the two chambers of Congress. Since 1912, there have been 435 people eligible to vote in the House of Representatives. However, over the years, there has been a shift in the proportion of members residing in each state. There must be at least one person elected from each state in the House of Representatives. After that, the number of representatives from each state is determined by the total number of residents in that state. According to the Constitution, the federal government is required to carry out a population census once every ten years to accurately count the number of residents living in each state. The census findings will be factored into a new formula that will determine the appropriate number of representatives for each state. For instance, if a state adds a significant number of citizens, that state may be eligible for one or more additional members. It is possible for that state to lose one or more people if they move to a different state. However, there will be no change to the overall number of representatives that have voting rights.

22. For how many years does a U.S. representative serve?

Right answer: 2

Explanation: The residents of a representative's district are known as the "constituents" of that representative. It is common practice for representatives to mirror the opinions of the people they represent. Constituents can vote lawmakers out of office if they do not comply with this demand. The Founding Fathers of the United States Constitution had the belief that having representatives serve terms of just two years and holding elections on a regular basis would keep them more in touch with their constituents and the public opinion as well as make them more aware of issues affecting their communities. The number of terms that a representative may serve in the House of Representatives is not restricted in any way by the Constitution. Every two years, every seat in the House of Representatives is up for election.

23. Name your U.S. Representative

Right answer: The answer will vary based on where the applicant lives. Note: District of Columbia residents and those living in U.S. territories should answer that D.C. (or the territory where they live) has no House representatives.

24. Whom does a U.S. Senator represent?

Right answer: All people in the state

Explanation: The people of a state elect senators to represent their interests in the Senate for a period of six years. Each of the two senators is responsible for representing all the state. Before the 17th Amendment to the Constitution was passed in 1913, state legislatures were responsible for selecting the individuals who would go on to serve as senators for their respective states. Now, each state's two senators are chosen directly by the citizens in that state.

25. Why do some states have more Representatives than other states?
Correct answers (choose one):
- Because of the state's population
- Because they have more people
- Because some states have more people

Explanation: The Founding Fathers wanted all of the people in each state to have an equal voice in government. The number of members that a state has in the House of Representatives is directly proportional to the population of that state. The House of Representatives is thus more responsive to the concerns of populous states. Every state has the same number of representatives in the Senate. This indicates that even states with a relatively low population nevertheless have a significant say in the decision-making process of the national government.

26. We elect a President to serve for how many years?
Right answer: 4

Explanation: The early founders of the United States of America believed the head of the British government, the monarch, had an excessive amount of authority. As a result of this, they constrained the authority of the new leader of the United States government. They concluded that the people should choose the president every four years via a vote. The only other figure in the United States to be chosen by popular vote rather than the Electoral College is the President. To choose who would serve as president of the United States, the authors of the Constitution established a system known as the Electoral College. A compromise was reached between having the president selected by Congress and having the president elected directly by the people. Citizens cast their ballots for electors, who then decide who will serve as president. Prior to the year 1951, there was no restriction placed on the number of terms that a president might serve. The 22nd Amendment to the Constitution stipulates that a president may serve for a maximum of two terms, each of which lasts for four years, for a combined total of eight years.

27. In what month do we vote for President?

Right answer: November

Explanation: The date of the national elections was not specified in the Constitution. In the past, elections for federal office were held on various days in each state that made up the country. In 1845, legislation was approved by Congress to establish a single day as the national voting day for all Americans. Because of this change, Election Day is now on the Tuesday after the first Monday of November. November was selected by Congress because most of the United States is rural. By the time November rolled around, farmers had finished their harvests and were free to cast their ballots. The forecast for the next week was another factor in deciding on this day. Because winter had not yet begun, people were free to travel. They selected Tuesday as the day of the election so that people would have a full day after the weekend to get to the polls.

28. What is the name of the President of the United States now?

Right answer: Joe Biden

29. Who currently holds the position of Vice President of the United States?

Right answer: Kamala Harris

30. If the President is unable to continue serving, who assumes the role of the President?

Right answer: The Vice President

Explanation: The Vice President automatically assumes the role of President if the incumbent is incapacitated, passes away, or resigns while still in office. Because of this, the requirements for the positions of Vice President and President are the same. In the history of the United States, nine times a Vice President was elevated to the position of President when the previous President passed away or resigned from office. In 1841, while still serving as President, William Henry Harrison passed away. In 1850, Zachary Taylor passed away while serving as President. In 1865, while still serving as President, Abraham Lincoln was assassinated. In 1881, James Garfield was assassinated while serving as President. William McKinley passed away while he was serving as President in 1901. 1923 was the year that Warren Harding passed away while in office. Franklin Roosevelt died in office in 1945. In 1963, President John F. Kennedy was assassinated while in office. In 1974, Richard Nixon announced his resignation from the presidency. There has never been a transition to the President led by anybody other than the Vice President.

31. If both the President and Vice President are unable to continue serving, who assumes the role of the President?

Right answer: The Speaker of the House

Explanation: If neither the President nor the Vice President can carry out their duties, the Speaker of the House of Representatives will assume the role. This has not always been the standard operating practice. Soon after the nation was established, a statute was enacted that elevated the position of the Senate President pro tempore to the position of third in line for the presidency, behind the President and the Vice President. When the Vice President is not present, the presidency of the Senate is passed on to the President Pro Tempore. In more recent times in American history, the secretary of state had the position of third in line. The Presidential Succession Act of 1947 brought Congress back to the original concept of having a legislative leader take the position of the next in line for the presidency. The 25th Amendment was finally passed in the year 1967. It outlined the processes that would be followed in the event of a presidential or vice-presidential vacancy.

32. Who is the Commander in Chief of the military?

Right answer: The President

Explanation: The Founding Fathers had a deep-seated commitment to the principles of republicanism. A republic is a form of government in which the political power of a nation derives from the people of that nation rather than from the rulers of that nation, and that political power is exercised by representatives who are chosen by the people. Because of this, they gave the role of commander in chief to the President. They sought a civilian who would be chosen by the whole population. They were adamant about not having a career military officer in charge. The armed forces are under the direction of the President, but only Congress has the authority to declare war and provide funds for the military. In 1973, a significant number of members of Congress believed the President was abusing or misusing the powers that came with his position as commander in chief. They believed that the president was disregarding the legislative branch and inhibiting the operation of the checks and balances system. The War Powers Act was enacted because of this reaction from Congress. The War Powers Act granted Congress a greater say in the decisions regarding the deployment of United States military forces. This law was vetoed by President Richard Nixon, but Congress was able to override his veto. Because we have a system of checks and balances, it is possible for one part of government to investigate the activities of other branches.

33. Who signs bills to become laws?

Right answer: The President

Explanation: A member of Congress, namely a senator (member of the Senate) or representative (member of the House of Representatives), is responsible for submitting a bill proposal at the beginning stages of the legislative process. The proposal is referred to as a "bill" after discussion on it has begun in either the Senate or the House. Following discussion in the Senate and House of Representatives, if a majority of members in both chambers vote to adopt the measure, it is sent to the President for his signature. If the President wants to see the measure passed into law, he will sign it. If the President does not want the measure to become law, he will use his veto power to stop the bill from passing. It is not possible for the President to initiate legislation. If he has an idea for a bill, he is required to approach a member of Congress for that bill to be introduced.

34. Who vetoes bills?

Right answer: The President

Explanation: The President has the right to veto legislation. This indicates that the President retains the authority to veto a law that has been approved by Congress. The President can stop a measure from being signed into law by using his or her veto power. The measure may be returned to Congress by the President in an unsigned state. Quite frequently, he will explain why he does not accept it. The President has ten days to make his decision about the law. After ten days, if the measure has not been signed by the President and Congress is still in session, the bill will become law without the President's signature. A "pocket veto" occurs when the President does nothing with the measure and Congress adjourns inside the 10-day timeframe; this results in the bill not becoming law and is known as a "dead letter." Even if the president does not sign the measure into law, it may become a law if two-thirds of both the House of Representatives and the Senate vote to approve it again. The phrase "overriding the president's veto" describes this procedure. It is not a simple task at all.

35. What does the President's Cabinet do?
Right answer: Advises the President

Explanation: The heads of the several executive departments are required to provide the President with advice according to the Constitution. The cabinet is made up of the heads of the many departments, most of whom are termed "secretaries." The cabinet members who will serve as the President's advisers are chosen by the President. It is necessary for most senators to vote in favor of a candidate before that person may be approved. It has always been within the President's power to alter the composition of the cabinet and to appoint new members to existing departments. For instance, when President George W. Bush first established the Department of Homeland Security, he immediately appointed a member of his cabinet to serve as the department's head.

36. Name two Cabinet-level positions
Correct answers (choose two):
- Secretary of Agriculture
- Secretary of Commerce
- Secretary of Defense
- Secretary of Education
- Secretary of Energy
- Secretary of Health and Human Services
- Secretary of Homeland Security
- Secretary of Housing and Urban Development
- Secretary of the Interior
- Secretary of Labor
- Secretary of State
- Secretary of Transportation
- Secretary of the Treasury
- Secretary of Veterans Affairs
- Attorney General
- Vice President

Explanation: According to the Constitution, the heads of the several executive agencies are obligated to give the President with recommendations. The cabinet is made up of the leaders of the many departments, the majority of whom are called "secretaries." The President is responsible for selecting the members of the cabinet who will act in the capacity of serving as the President's advisors. Before a candidate can be authorized, there has to be support from the majority of senators in order for the vote to go in their favor. It has traditionally been the prerogative of the President to make changes to the cabinet and appoint new members to the various departments that already exist. For example, when President George W. Bush originally founded the Department of Homeland Security, he promptly chose a member of his cabinet to serve as the department's director. This individual is now serving in that capacity.

37. What does the judicial branch do?
Correct answers (choose one):
- Decides if a law goes against the Constitution
- Explains laws
- Resolves disputes (disagreements)

- Reviews laws

Explanation: One of the three pillars that make up the United States government is the judicial system. The Judicial Branch of the United States Government is comprised of the Supreme Court, which was established by the Constitution. The other federal courts were established by Congress. The judicial branch is comprised of each one of these courts. The courts are responsible for analyzing the laws, providing explanations for them, and mediating disputes that arise about the interpretation of the laws. The Constitution is the guiding document for the decisions made by the Supreme Court of the United States. The Supreme Court has the authority to declare a statute unconstitutional if it determines that the law violates the Constitution in any way. In this instance, the legislation is struck down by the court. The United States Supreme Court is the court of last resort for all issues involving compliance with federal laws and international treaties. In addition to that, it renders decisions on other instances, such as disputes between states.

38. What is the highest court in the United States?
Right answer: The Supreme Court

Explanation: The Supreme Court of the United States presides over all other federal courts and has unquestioned power over them. The decisions that it makes have a big impact. A decision made by the Supreme Court might have repercussions for several pending matters in the subordinate courts. The decisions of the Supreme Court about how the Constitution and federal statutes should be interpreted are final. The authority that the Supreme Court has over the states is severely restricted. It does not have the authority to decide issues pertaining to state law or state constitutions. The Supreme Court has the authority to rule that state legislation or action violates either federal law or the Constitution of the United States of America. If this occurs, the law of the state can no longer be enforced. This authority, often known as "judicial review," was created by the decision made by the Supreme Court in the case Marbury v. Madison. Cases involving substantial social and public policy problems, which impact every American, are also heard and decided by the Supreme Court. The decision of the United States Supreme Court in the case Brown v. the Board of Education of Topeka put an end to the practice of racial segregation in public schools.

39. How many justices are on the Supreme Court?
Right answer: Nine Justices

40. Who currently holds the position of Chief Justice of the United States?
Right answer: John Roberts

41. Name one power of the federal government.
Correct answers (choose one):
- To print money
- To declare war
- To create an army
- To make treaties

Explanation: The federal government and the state governments each have some of the authorities, but the federal government has the majority. The United States federal government is an example of a limited government. Its powers are limited to those that are outlined in the Constitution of the United States of America. The federal government is granted the authority to issue money, declare war, organize an army, and negotiate treaties with foreign countries, all by virtue of the Constitution. Most powers not specifically granted to the federal government in the Constitution are delegated to the state governments.

42. Name one power of the states
Correct answers (choose one):

- Approve zoning and land use
- Give a driver's license
- Provide protection (police)
- Provide safety (fire departments)
- Provide schooling and education

Explanation: The federal and state governments have authority in the United States. Before the adoption of the Constitution, each of the 13 colonies had its own independent government, quite like modern state governments. The Articles of Confederation and the Constitution are the documents that laid the groundwork for the establishment of a national or federal government. Today, even though every state has its own constitution, such state constitutions may not be in direct opposition to the Constitution of the United States. The United States Constitution is the highest legal authority in the nation. The Constitution of the United States grants the state governments with some rights that are not delegated to the federal government. The ability to set traffic restrictions, marriage requirements, and the conditions for obtaining a driver's license are some of the authorities that the state government has. In addition, the Constitution includes a rundown of the authorities that are expressly denied to the states. For instance, state governments are not permitted to "coin" (create) their own currencies. There are also other authorities that are shared by the state and federal governments, such as the capacity to tax individuals.

43. Who is the Governor of your state now?
Right answer: The answer will vary based on where the applicant lives (D.C. residents should answer that D.C. doesn't have a governor).

44. What is the capital of your state?
Right answer: The answer will vary based on where the applicant lives (D.C. residents should answer that D.C. isn't a state and therefore doesn't have a capital. Residents of U.S. territories must name the capital of their territory).

45. Name two major political parties in the United States.
Right answer: Democratic and Republican

Explanation: The political parties we have today were not outlined in the Constitution. They were particularly cautioned not to do so by former President George Washington. Almost immediately after the nation's founding, two distinct political parties emerged. Both the Democratic-Republicans and the Federalists belonged to this group. The Democratic Party and the Republican Party are now the two main political parties in the United States. The Democratic Party sprang from the Democratic-Republican Party under the leadership of President Andrew Jackson. In the 1860s, the Republican Party succeeded the Whig Party as the largest political party in the United States. Abraham Lincoln was the first President elected by the Republican Party. There have been several other parties throughout the history of the United States. The Know-Nothing Party, also known as the American Party, the Bull-Moose Party, also known as the Progressive Party, the Reform Party, and the Green Party were among these parties in the past. They have participated in American politics in a variety of capacities. In the United States, joining a political party is entirely up to the individual. People who have similar political beliefs band together to form political parties to advance their candidates for elected office and their points of view about public policy.

46. What is the political party of the President now?
Right answer: Democratic Party

47. Who currently holds the position of Speaker of the House of Representatives?
Right answer: Kevin McCarthy

C: Rights and Responsibilities

48. Describe one of the four amendments to the Constitution about who can vote
Correct answers (choose one):
- Individuals of any gender and race, who are citizens, have the right to vote.
- Every citizen is eligible to vote.
- Citizens who are 18 years old or older can vote.
- Voting does not require the payment of a poll tax.

Explanation: One of the most essential duties of being a citizen in the United States is exercising one's right to vote. People in a democratic society get to vote for the officials who will represent their interests in government. Regarding voting, the Constitution has been amended four times. The 15th Amendment to the Constitution of the United States grants voting rights to American males of any color. It wasn't until after the Civil War and the abolition of slavery that it was written. The right of women to vote was established by the 19th Amendment. It was a direct consequence of the struggle for the right of women to vote, sometimes known as the women's rights movement. Following the adoption of the 15th Amendment, the leaders of many southern states expressed displeasure with the fact that African Americans now had the right to vote. These leaders devised fines known as poll taxes with the intention of discouraging citizens from using their right to vote. Because of the 24th Amendment, these poll taxes are no longer permissible. The voting age was decreased from 21 to 18 with the passage of the 26th Amendment.

49. Name one responsibility that is only for US citizens
Correct answers (choose one):
- Participate as a juror.
- Exercise the right to vote in federal elections.

Explanation: Citizens of the United States have the duties of both serving on juries and voting in federal elections at some point in their lives. The right to a trial by jury is guaranteed to all people under the Constitution. The members of the jury are all citizens of the United States. A citizen jury may assist in guaranteeing that a trial is conducted in an impartial manner. Voting is another significant obligation that is placed on individuals. Voting is a highly vital aspect of any democracy, even though individuals are not required by law to exercise this right. Voting is the most fundamental way that people may take part in the political process. residents cast their votes for those they believe will best represent them and their perspectives, and those leaders then work to further the residents' best interests.

50. Name one right only for United States citizens.
Correct answers (choose one):
- Vote in a federal election
- Run for federal office

Explanation: Voting in federal elections is a right guaranteed to all citizens of the United States. In elections for municipal or state offices that do not require voters to be citizens of the United States, permanent residents have the right to vote. Voting in federal elections is restricted to only citizens of the United States. Candidates for federal office must be citizens of the United States. One of the requirements to meet to be eligible for election to either the Senate or the House of Representatives is the required number of years spent as a citizen of the United States. To run for Senate, one must have been a citizen of the United States for a minimum of nine years. A citizen of the United States for a minimum of seven years is required to run for a seat in the House of Representatives. A citizen of the United States who was not born in the country is not eligible to run for the office of president of the United States. Citizens of the United States are expected to uphold certain obligations and enjoy the privileges that come with citizenship. These include adhering to the law, maintaining an awareness of current events, participating in political processes, and paying taxes.

51. Name two rights of everyone living in the U.S.
Correct answers:
- Freedom of assembly
- Freedom of expression
- Freedom of religion
- Freedom of speech
- Freedom to petition the government
- The right to bear arms

Explanation: According to what Thomas Jefferson had to say about the matter, "[The] best principles [of our republic] secure to all its citizens a perfect equality of rights." In search of a better life, millions of people have made the journey to the United States. Many of these rights are guaranteed to every individual who resides inside the United States under the Constitution and the Bill of Rights. Freedom of expression, freedom of religion, freedom of speech, and the right to carry weapons are all included in this category of rights. Paying taxes and following the law are only two of the numerous responsibilities that come with citizenship in the United States, which are shared by all persons who live in the country.

52. What do we express loyalty to when reciting the Pledge of Allegiance?
Correct answers:
- The United States
- The flag

Explanation: The flag of the United States is a significant representation of the nation. The phrase "I pledge allegiance to the Flag of the United States of America and to the Republic for which it stands, one Nation, under God, indivisible, with liberty and justice for all" is included in the "Pledge of Allegiance" that is said in front of the flag. When we recite the Pledge of Allegiance, we traditionally place our right hand on our hearts while facing the flag. The vow was written by Francis Bellamy. It was written specifically for youngsters to recite on the anniversary of Christopher Columbus's discovery of America and was originally published in The Youth's Companion magazine in 1892. On June 22, 1942, Congress gave the commitment its formal acknowledgment. Since it was written in 1892, there have been two modifications made to it. It was modified from "I pledge allegiance to my flag" to "I pledge allegiance to the Flag of the United States of America." On June 14, 1954, Congress added "under God" to the pledge.

53. Name one promise you make when you become a U.S citizen.
- Demonstrate loyalty to the United States
- Defend the Laws and Constitution of the United States
- Renounce allegiance to any other countries
- Abide by the laws of the United States
- Serve the nation by undertaking significant work when necessary
- Serve in the U.S. military if required

Explanation: The Constitution of the United States provided Congress the authority to adopt a standard naturalization system when the United States of America became an independent nation. The process through which immigrants may eventually become citizens was codified by Congress. There are a number of these conditions that are still in effect today, such as the necessity to have lived in the United States for a certain amount of time, the requirement to have a morally upstanding character, and the demand to be aware of and adhere to the Constitution's guiding ideas. The last stage in the process for an immigrant to become a citizen of the United States is to attend a naturalization ceremony where they will be required to swear an oath of allegiance to the United States. The Oath of Allegiance states, "I hereby declare, on oath, that I absolutely and entirely renounce and abjure all allegiance and fidelity to any foreign prince, potentate, state, or sovereignty of whom or which I have heretofore been a subject or citizen; that I will support and defend the Constitution and laws of the United States of America against all enemies, foreign and domestic; that I will bear true faith and allegiance to the same; that I will bear arms on behalf of the United States when required by the law; that I will perform noncombatant service in the Armed Forces of the United States when required by the law; that I will perform work of national importance under civilian direction when required by the law; and that I take this obligation freely without any mental reservation or purpose of evasion; so help me God."

54. What age do citizens have to be to vote for President?
Right answer: 18 and older

Explanation: To vote in elections in the United States, citizens need to be at least 21 years old during most of the country's history. During the 1960s and 1970s, while the Vietnam War was going on, many people had the idea that those who were old enough to fight in a war should also be old enough to vote in that war. This was a common sentiment. Following the passage of the 26th Amendment in 1971, the voting age requirement was lowered from 21 to 18 years old for all federal, state, and municipal elections. People were able to register to vote with less effort because to a law that was passed in 1993 called the National Voter Registration Act. Voter registration is now available to individuals via the mail, at public assistance offices, and when they apply for or renew their driver's licenses.

55. Name two ways that US Citizens can participate in their democracy
Correct answers (choose two):
- Call senators and representatives
- Give an elected official your opinion on an issue
- Help with a campaign
- Join a civic group
- Join a community group
- Join a political party

- Publicly support or oppose an issue or policy
- Run for office
- Vote
- Write to a newspaper

Explanation: Citizens are expected to participate in the life of their communities. The health and vitality of democracy are directly linked to the level of participation of its citizens in political processes. There are numerous ways individuals may become engaged. They may assist new immigrants learn English and civics as a volunteer, join the Parent Teacher Association (PTA) of their child's school, run for a seat on the local school board, or volunteer to work at a voting station. Other options include joining the Parent Teacher Association (PTA) of their child's school. Voting, volunteering for a political campaign, joining a civic or community group, or calling one's senator or representative to discuss an issue that is important to them are other ways for individuals to make their voices heard on critical matters.

56. What is the last day you can submit federal income tax forms?
Right answer: April 15

Explanation: Every year, the 15th of April is usually the latest day you may file your federal income tax return with the Internal Revenue Service. The Constitution gave the federal government the authority to levy and collect taxes. Money is necessary for the federal government to pay off the nation's obligations, protect the country, and meet the requirements of its citizens. When the nation was young, it was difficult to obtain money from the initial 13 states. This made it challenging to fund important projects. The Revenue Act of 1861 was the first time the federal government began taxing individual income. This was only a stopgap measure. In 1894, a federal income tax with a flat rate was passed into law; however, the Supreme Court later ruled that this was unconstitutional. The 16th Amendment was finally approved the next year in 1913. It granted Congress the authority to levy taxes on individual income. The term "taxable income" refers to money produced today through a variety of sources, including wages, self-employment, tips, and the sale of property. These taxes are used by the government to ensure the safety and security of our nation. In addition, it conducts research with the goal of curing and preventing illnesses. In addition, the government is responsible for the insurance of our money held in banks, the education of both children and adults, and the construction and maintenance of our roads and highways. All of these and a great deal more may be paid for using tax revenue.

57. When must all men register for the Selective Service?
Correct answers (choose one):
- At 18
- Between 18 and 26

Explanation: During the Civil War, President Abraham Lincoln attempted to conscript individuals to fight, but this was met with widespread resistance and even some rioting. The Selective Service Act was voted into law by Congress in 1917. During World War I, President Woodrow Wilson was granted the authority under this legislation to temporarily augment the size of the United States military. The Selective Training and Service Act was signed into law by President Franklin D. Roosevelt in 1940, which led to establishing the very first draft at a period of relative calm. This event marked the beginning of what is now known as the Selective Service System in the United States. In both the Korean and Vietnam wars, there was a renewed necessity for the draft. There is no longer a mandatory military conscription in the United States; nonetheless, all males between the ages of 18 and 26 are required by law to register with the Selective Service System. When a man signs up for the draft, he informs the government that he is willing to serve in any of the branches of the

United States Armed Forces. He has the option of registering in person at a post office in the United States or online.

American History

A: Colonial Period and Independence

58. Name one reason colonists came to America.

Correct answers (choose one):

- Freedom
- Political liberty
- Religious freedom
- Economic opportunity
- Practice their religion
- Escape persecution

Explanation: Colonists from England and other European nations traveled over the Atlantic Ocean to settle in what would become the American colonies in the 1600s and 1700s. Some people fled Europe to avoid being restricted in their religious practices or persecuted for their faith and to be able to do so freely. Many people came in search of economic opportunities, while others were looking for political freedom. These kinds of liberties and possibilities often were not afforded to colonists in their respective nations of origin. The American colonies represented an opportunity for independence and a fresh start for these early colonists. These are still some of the primary draws for immigration to the United States in the modern era.

59. Who inhabited America prior to the arrival of Europeans?

Correct answers (choose one):

- American Indians
- Native Americans

Explanation: When the Pilgrims first landed in America, the continent was already home to several powerful American Indian nations, including the Navajo, Sioux, Cherokee, and Iroquois. The Wampanoag were the native inhabitants of the region when the Pilgrims established their colony there. The Wampanoag people were the ones who taught the Pilgrims crucial life lessons, such as how to farm using a variety of techniques and how to cultivate foods like maize, beans, and squash. As more Europeans immigrated to North America and settled in western regions, tensions rose in relations with some American Indian communities, leading to violent encounters on occasion. In the end, after much bloodshed, the settlers prevailed against those American Indian tribes and stole a large portion of the land that belonged to them.

60. Which group of people was taken to the U.S. and sold as slaves?

Correct answers (choose one):

- Africans

- People from Africa

Explanation: Long before the United States of America was established, slavery was practiced in several other nations. By the year 1700, numerous people from Africa were being transported to the American colonies to work as slaves. Everyone had their free will taken away from them. When they were bought and sold as slaves, they were often torn away from their relatives. Slaves were forced to labor without compensation and were denied their most fundamental rights. Although the majority worked in agriculture, slaves in the colonies were also put to work in a wide variety of other occupations. The institution of slavery presented a problem for the development of a society based on the principles of individual liberty and democratic governance. It was a primary contributor to the outbreak of the American Civil War.

61. What was the reason behind the colonists' fight against the British?

Correct answers (choose one):
- Excessive taxes imposed without representation (taxation without representation)
- Because the British army occupied their homes
- Because they didn't have self-government

Explanation: Before the start of the American Revolutionary War in 1775, the fury felt by the American colonists had been building for years. The option to declare independence from Great Britain was one that was not taken lightly by most of the colonists. However, as stated in the Declaration of Independence, the "repeated injuries" that Great Britain inflicted against the Americans was a major factor in convincing many people to join the revolt. The British imposed taxes on the colonists without obtaining their permission, and the colonists had no one to speak for their interests and beliefs in front of the British government. They were also enraged by the fact that the colonists were compelled to give British troops access to their houses for the purposes of eating and sleeping. The colonists were under the impression that the British did not respect their constitutionally guaranteed rights. The British ruled the colonists without obtaining their approval, preventing them from exercising their right to self-government.

62. Who wrote the Declaration of Independence?

Right answer: Thomas Jefferson

Explanation: In 1776, Thomas Jefferson was the primary author of the Declaration of Independence. He was a highly influential political theorist as well as a political leader. The Declaration of Independence contains several principles that are very significant to the structure and functioning of the American government, such as the notion that all people are created equal. People are born with specific rights, such as the right to life, the right to liberty, and the right to pursue happiness. This is another fundamental concept. Between the years 1801 and 1809, Jefferson served as the third President of the United States of America. Jefferson served as both the governor of Virginia and the first secretary of state of the United States before he was elected president. He was a staunch advocate for individual rights, most notably the ability to practice one's faith. Jefferson fought for the preservation of these liberties. Because of this, he was not interested in having a robust national government.

63. When was the Declaration of Independence officially adopted?
Right answer: July 4, 1776

Explanation: The first meeting of the Continental Congress took place in Philadelphia, Pennsylvania, in 1774, and it was attended by delegates from 12 of the 13 colonies. Only Georgia was not included among the first 13 colonies. These delegates were upset with the legislation in Britain that discriminated against them in some way. They started gathering people together to form an army. After hostilities had broken out between the colonies and the British Army in 1775, the Second Continental Congress was called into session. The Continental Congress gave the task of writing the Declaration of Independence to Thomas Jefferson and several other delegates. After finishing his draft of the Declaration of Independence, Thomas Jefferson gave it to John Adams, Benjamin Franklin, and the other members of the committee so that they could go over it and make any necessary changes. Following the completion of the committee's work to make modifications, the Declaration was then read aloud to the whole of Congress. Declaring the colonies' independence from England was the primary goal of the Declaration of Independence (Declaration). In the Declaration of Independence, it was declared that the people can establish a new government if an existing government fails to respect the rights of its citizens. The colonists severed their ties with their British overlords as a result of this cause. The Declaration of Independence was approved for public circulation on July 4, 1776, by the Second Continental Congress.

64. Name three of the 13 original states
Correct answers (choose three):
- New Hampshire
- Massachusetts
- Rhode Island
- Connecticut
- New York
- New Jersey
- Pennsylvania
- Delaware
- Maryland
- Virginia
- North Carolina
- South Carolina
- Georgia

Explanation: All of the first 13 states had their beginnings as British colonies. In 1776, representatives from each of these colonies convened a meeting at which they proclaimed their independence from Great Britain. Following the conclusion of the American Revolutionary War, the colonies successfully transitioned into free and sovereign states. Following the transformation of the 13 colonies into states, each state established its own administration. They penned the constitutions of the states. At some point in time, the people living in these states came up with a fresh concept for a national government that would eventually consolidate all the states into a single country under the

Constitution of the United States. Delaware, Pennsylvania, and New Jersey were the first three colonies to become states after their independence from Britain. This took place in the year 1787. In 1788, eight of the colonies eventually became states. These states were Georgia, Connecticut, Massachusetts, Maryland, South Carolina, New Hampshire, and Virginia . New York was also included in the list. In 1789, North Carolina was admitted to the union as a state. In 1790, Rhode Island was admitted to the union as a state. Even though the colonies were acknowledged as states after the signing of the Declaration of Independence, the date on which they became states is determined by the date on which they ratified (accepted) the Constitution of the United States. There are now fifty states that make up the United States.

65. What happened at the Constitutional Convention?
Correct answers (choose one):
- The Constitution was written.
- The Founding Fathers wrote the Constitution.

Explanation: Philadelphia, Pennsylvania, served as the host city for the Constitutional Convention, which ran from May through September of 1787. To improve the Articles of Confederation, 55 delegates from 12 of the original 13 states (except Rhode Island) got together and worked on the problem. The reason for the gathering of the delegates was the widespread disapproval of the Articles among the American leaders. The Articles of Confederation led to a weak national government that was unable to effectively carry out its duties. Instead of amending the Articles of Confederation, the delegates concluded that a new governing text with a more robust national government should be drafted. This document would be called the Constitution. Each state was required to send delegates, and throughout the four months that they toiled away behind closed doors on the new treaty, they encouraged free and open debate. "The Framers" are the people who attended the Constitutional Convention and are referred to by that name. On September 17, 1787, 39 delegates signed the new Constitution, making it official.

66. When was the Constitution written?
Right answer: 1787

Explanation: A new form of government for the United States of America was established with the writing of the Constitution in 1787; this form of government is still in use today. James Madison is generally regarded as the primary author of the Constitution. The United States of America elected him as its fourth president. Although it is just a few pages long, the Constitution of the United States of America outlines the guiding principles of the United States government as well as the rights of its inhabitants. The paper is divided into seven articles and a prologue. The Constitution has been revised or amended a total of 27 times since it was first ratified. For the Constitution to become legally binding, it needed to be ratified by three-fourths of the states (9 out of the original 13). On December 7, 1787, the state of Delaware became the first in the union to ratify the Constitution. New Hampshire was the ninth state to ratify the Constitution when it did so in the year 1788. The Constitution was put into effect on March 4, 1789, the same day that the first meeting of Congress took place. In the same year, George Washington was sworn in as the nation's first president. The Constitution had been approved by each of the original 13 states by the year 1790.

67. Name one of the writers of the Federalist Papers.
Correct answers (name one):
- (James) Madison
- (Alexander) Hamilton
- (John) Jay
- Publius

Explanation: The Federalist Papers were a collection of 85 articles that were published in New York newspapers at the time when the state of New York was debating whether to endorse the Constitution of the United States of America. The writings were written in 1787 and 1788 under the pen name "Publius" by Alexander Hamilton, John Jay, and James Madison. The essays provided justification for ratifying the Constitution on the part of the state. During the time when other states were debating whether to ratify the Constitution, the writings were also published in other newspapers outside of New York. In the year 1788, the writings were collected into a single volume and given the title The Federalist. Even in modern times, individuals continue to study the Federalist Papers to better comprehend the Constitution.

68. Name one thing Benjamin Franklin is famous for.
Correct answers (name one):
- U.S. diplomat
- The oldest member of the Constitutional Convention
- First Postmaster General of the United States
- Writer of "Poor Richard's Almanac"
- Started the first free libraries

Explanation: Benjamin Franklin is widely regarded as one of the Founding Fathers of the United States who had the greatest impact on the nation's development. He was one of the signers of the United States Constitution and the oldest person to serve as a delegate to the Constitutional Convention. He worked as a printer, novelist, politician, diplomat, and inventor in addition to being a diplomat. By the time he was in his mid-20s, he had already achieved success as a printer and had begun producing books and articles. Poor Richard's Almanac was Benjamin Franklin's most well-known publication. Additionally, he established the first library in the United States. Its members shared books with one another by lending them out. He was actively involved in the political life of the colony. As a diplomat for the United States, he also spent a lot of time in England and France. Franklin was given the position of first postmaster general by the Second Continental Congress in the year 1775.

69. Who is considered the "Father of Our Country"?
Right answer: (George) Washington

Explanation: Many people refer to George Washington as the Father of Our Country. He was the first President of the United States. Before that, he had a distinguished career as a valiant commander who won the American Revolutionary War for the Continental Army by leading them to victory over Great Britain. Following his triumph over the British Army, George Washington withdrew to the property he had called Mount Vernon in the state of Virginia. He gave up his retirement to participate in the formation of the new nation's political structure. In 1787, he served as the head of the Constitutional Convention that was held in Philadelphia.

70. Who was the first president?
Right answer: (George) Washington

Explanation: The first President of the United States to hold the office was George Washington. In 1789, he took office for the first time. The year 1793 marked the beginning of his second tenure in office. Washington was an important figure in the formation of the new country and was a strong proponent of American unification. He was also instrumental in shaping the modern President of the United States. After serving two terms as president, he made the decision to step down willingly. By willingly ceding power, he set a good example for future leaders in his own nation as well as in other countries throughout the globe. The custom in the United States of a president serving no more than two terms remained until Franklin D. Roosevelt, who was elected to office four times (1933–1945). Before Roosevelt, no president had served more than two terms. The current restriction of two terms in office for the president was established by the 22nd Amendment to the Constitution, which was ratified in 1947.

B: 1800s

71. Which territory did the United States acquire from France in 1803 through a purchase?
Correct answers (choose one):
- The Louisiana Territory
- Louisiana

Explanation: The land located to the west of the Mississippi River was known as the Louisiana Territory. It had a total area of 828,000 square miles. In 1803, the United States of America paid France $15 million to purchase the Louisiana Territory from them. On April 30, 1803, the Treaty of Purchase and Sale of the Louisiana Territory was signed in Paris. It was the greatest purchase of land in the annals of United States history. Farmers were now able to carry their agricultural goods down the Mississippi River without first obtaining permission from neighboring nations. This was significant because New Orleans was a major maritime port in the United States. The size of the United States was effectively increased and stretched westward because of the Louisiana Purchase. William Clark and Meriwether Lewis were the leaders of the expedition that mapped the Louisiana Territory.

72. Name one war fought by the U.S. in the 1800s.
Correct answers (choose one):
- Civil War
- Mexican-American War
- Spanish-American War
- War of 1812

Explanation: During the 1800s, the United States engaged in important conflicts such as the War of 1812, the Mexican-American War, the American Civil War, and the Spanish-American War. The years 1812 through 1815 were the years when the War of 1812 was fought. James Madison, who was serving as President at the time, requested that Congress declare war on Great Britain. The British were preventing American ships from sailing and capturing them. They also provided American Indians with weapons so they could battle against the Americans. Because of this battle, there was a disruption in the nation's commerce, and the Capitol building in the United States was destroyed. The conflict was ultimately won by the Americans. After the Revolutionary War, the United States of America was forced to defend its independence from a foreign nation for the very first time during this conflict. The Mexican-American War was a struggle that took place between the United States of America and Mexico. In the year 1846, fighting first broke out in Texas. General Zachary Taylor and the men under his command were given orders by President James Polk to seize territory that was being claimed by both the United States and Mexico. Polk had the view that it was essential for the growth of the United States to continue its westward migration. Following an invasion by Mexico, the United States of America declared war on Mexico. The United States and Mexico signed the Treaty of Guadalupe Hidalgo in February of 1848, which marked the end of the conflict between the two countries. The United States gained possession of Texas because of this treaty, which also expanded the country's borders westward to include the Pacific Ocean. During the time of the Civil War, the citizens of the United States fought against one another on opposing sides. During the Civil War, citizens of the northern states of the United States fought on the side of the federal government (also known as "the Union") against citizens of the southern states. The southern states were actively working toward secession to establish a new country known as the Confederate States of America (often referred to simply as "the Confederacy"). The conflict began in 1861 and continued until 1865, when the Confederate army finally capitulated and surrendered to the Union army. During the course of the American Civil War, a great number of lives were taken. During the Spanish-American War, which began in 1898, the United States fought against Spain. Since the United States had vested economic interests in Cuba, it was in the best interests of the United States to assist Cuba in achieving independence from Spain. The conflict started when a warship belonging to the United States was sunk close to Cuba. Many Americans were under the impression that the ship had been assaulted by Spanish pirates. Because of this factor, the United States went to war with Spain. At the close of 1898, the United States had emerged victorious from their participation in the war. After Cuba achieved its freedom, the United States gained control of Guam, Puerto Rico, and the Philippines, and these regions were referred to as territories.

73. Name the U.S. war between the North and the South
Correct answers (choose one):
- The Civil War
- The War between the States

Explanation: The conflict that became known as the American Civil War is often referred to as the War between the States. It was a conflict between the people who lived in the states in the north and those who lived in the states in the south. Although the American Civil War took place in several different locations around the country, the majority of the fighting took place in the southern states. The conflict started at Fort Sumter, which was in South Carolina. In July of 1861, the northern (Union) army and the southern (Confederate) army engaged in the first major combat of the American Civil War at Bull Run, near Manassas, Virginia. The Union anticipated a speedy conclusion to the conflict. After suffering a crushing setback at the Battle of Bull Run, the Union quickly came to the realization that the war would be protracted and challenging. Richmond, Virginia, the capital of the Confederacy, was taken by Union forces in 1865, marking the end of the American Civil War. At Appomattox Courthouse, located in central Virginia, Union army Lieutenant General Ulysses S. Grant accepted the unconditional surrender of Confederate army General Robert E. Lee. More than three million individuals from the United States participated in the conflict that lasted for four years, and it claimed the lives of more than 600,000 people.

74. Name one problem that led to the Civil War

Correct answers (choose one):

- Slavery
- Economic reasons
- States' rights

Explanation: The American Civil War started when 11 southern states decided to break away from the United States and create their own nation, which came to be known as the Confederate States of America. These southern states thought their freedom to make their own judgments was being endangered by the federal authority of the United States. They desired for each state to have the ability to make its own choices about its governance and to have states' rights. If the national government disagreed with the state government, then they did not want to obey the national government. Both the North and the South operated their economies in quite different ways. Slave labor was an essential component of the agriculturally oriented South Carolina economy. The southern states of the United States had the concern that the federal government would put an end to slavery. The southern states believed this would be detrimental to both their economic and political autonomy. The economy of the northern states was less dependent on slavery and had a greater amount of industrialization. The states in the northern region of the United States waged war to preserve the Union as a single nation. They tried to prevent the southern states from forming a new country affiliated with the Confederacy. In addition, there were a lot of individuals living up north who were against keeping slaves. These disagreements paved the way for the American Civil War, which began in 1861 and continued until 1865.

75. Name one important thing that Abraham Lincoln did.

Correct answers (choose one):

- Freed the slaves (Emancipation Proclamation)
- Saved (or preserved) the Union
- Led the U.S. during the Civil War

Explanation: During his tenure as President of the United States, which spanned from 1861 through 1865, Abraham Lincoln was also the nation's commander in chief during the American Civil War. Lincoln believed that the secession of the southern states into the Confederacy violated the Constitution, and he desired to maintain the integrity of the Union. He released The Emancipation Proclamation in 1863, in the middle of the American Civil War. It made the proclamation that the slaves who had been living in the states that had rebelled against the Union were now free forever. In addition, Abraham Lincoln is well-known for the "Gettysburg Address." In November of 1863, he delivered the address at the town of Gettysburg, in the state of Pennsylvania. In the earlier part of that year, at the Battle of Gettysburg, the northern (Union) army had prevailed over the Confederate army to prevent the latter from invading the Northern territories. In remembrance of the numerous soldiers who lost their lives during this conflict, the Governor of Pennsylvania erected the Gettysburg Soldiers' National Cemetery. At the ceremony of dedication, Lincoln gave a speech in which he lauded those who had fought and lost their lives in war. He pleaded for those who were still alive to recommit themselves to the cause of preserving the Union to ensure that "government of the people, by the people, and for the people shall not perish from the earth." John Wilkes Booth, a supporter of the Confederacy, assassinated Abraham Lincoln at Ford's Theatre in Washington, District of Columbia, on April 14, 1865, not long after Lincoln had been inaugurated for his second term as president.

76. What did the Emancipation Proclamation do?
Correct answers (choose one):

- Freed the slaves
- Freed slaves in the Confederacy
- Freed slaves in the Confederate states
- Freed slaves in most Southern states

Explanation: The Emancipation Proclamation was released by President Abraham Lincoln in the year 1863, right in the thick of the American Civil War. The Emancipation Proclamation said that all slaves who had been residing in states that were part of the Confederacy were now free. A significant number of slaves enlisted in the Union army. The American Civil War ended in 1865, and the people who had been enslaved in the South were able to maintain their freedom. The 13th Amendment to the Constitution, which abolished slavery across the whole country of the United States, was a direct result of the Emancipation Proclamation.

77. What did Susan B. Anthony do?
Correct answers (choose one):

- Fought for women's rights
- Fought for civil rights

Explanation: On February 15, 1820, Susan B. Anthony made her debut in the world in Massachusetts. Her work advocating for the suffrage of women earned her a lot of attention. She took a vocal stance against slavery and advocated for women's rights to be treated equally in the workplace. The right to vote was extended to women under the United States Constitution with the passing of the 19th Amendment in 1920. Susan B. Anthony had passed away 14 years prior to the 19th Amendment being ratified, yet despite this, it was still often referred to as the Susan B. Anthony Amendment. In 1979, she made history by being the first woman to have her portrait included on a United States coin that was in circulation. The name of the coin is the Susan B. Anthony dollar, and it has a face value of one dollar.

C: Recent American History

78. Name one war fought by the United States in the 1900s.
Correct answers (choose one):

- (Persian) Gulf War
- Korean War
- Vietnam War
- World War I
- World War II

Explanation: World War I, World War II, the Korean War, the Vietnam War, and the (Persian) Gulf War were the five conflicts that the United States participated in during the 1900s. 1914 marked the beginning of World War I. After German submarines attacked ships belonging to the United Kingdom and the United States in 1917, and after Germany approached Mexico about beginning a war against the United States, the United States joined the conflict. In 1918, the Allied Powers, headed by Britain, France, and the United States, were victorious against the Central Powers, who were led by Germany, Austria-Hungary, and the Ottoman Empire. This resulted in the conclusion of the war. 1919 was the year that formally marked the conclusion of World War I according to the Treaty of Versailles. The phrase "the war to end all wars" was often used to refer to World War I.

When Germany invaded Poland in 1939, this marked the beginning of World War II. The next step was the declaration of war against Germany by France and Great Britain. Together, Germany, Italy, and Japan comprised what came to be known as the Axis powers during World War II. After the Japanese assault on Pearl Harbor in Hawaii in 1941, the United States of America officially joined World War II. The United States of America, together with France and Great Britain, was in command of the Allied invasion of France in 1944, which came to be known as "D-Day." By May of 1945, the process of freeing Europe from the control of Germany was finished. The surrender of Japan in August of 1945 was the event that finally brought an end to World War II.

When the North Korean Army crossed the 38th parallel into South Korean territory in 1950, this marked the beginning of the Korean War. After the end of World War II, a new border was established at the 38th parallel. This barrier divided the southern region of Korea, which was aligned with the United States, from the northern region of Korea, which was dominated by the communist party. During this time, the United States was lending assistance to build a democratic government in South Korea. The United States of America offered its assistance in the form of military might to halt the progression of the North Korean Army. During the Korean War, democratic countries squared up against communist regimes in direct confrontation. The Korean War lasted from 1950 to 1953, during which time it resulted in the formation of the nations of North Korea and South Korea.

In the conflict known as the Vietnam War, which lasted from 1959 through 1975, the United States Armed Forces and the South Vietnamese Army battled against the North Vietnamese. The democratic administration in the south of the nation received assistance from the United States of America to withstand the pressure from the communist north. Following the conclusion of the war in 1975, the nation was provisionally divided between the communist-controlled North Vietnam and the democratic South Vietnam. In 1976, Vietnam was completely governed by communist party officials. As a direct consequence of the Vietnam War, around 60,000 service members of the United States Armed Forces died or went missing.

The invasion of Kuwait by Iraq on August 2nd, 1990 marked the beginning of the Persian Gulf War. As a result of this assault, the Iraqi Army was brought closer to Saudi Arabia and its oil deposits, which provided a significant portion of the world's supply of oil. The United States of America and a great number of other nations had the goal of driving the Iraqi Army out of Kuwait and stopping it from attacking other countries in the area. The United States led a multinational coalition of troops authorized by the United Nations into action against the Iraqi Army in January 1991 under the direction of the United Nations. After just a month of fighting, the coalition was successful in expelling Iraqi forces from Kuwait. On February 28, 1991, the coalition announced that it would be ceasing hostilities.

79. Who was President during World War I?
Right answer: (Woodrow) Wilson

Explanation: Woodrow Wilson served as the 28th President of the United States from 1913 through 1921. During his first time in office, he tried to prevent the United States from becoming involved in World War I. By 1917, Wilson was aware that this objective could no longer be achieved, therefore he requested that Congress declare war on Germany. On January 8, 1918, he gave a speech to Congress in which he outlined the "Fourteen Points" that justified the war and asked for a plan to keep peace after the war. When asked why the United States participated in the war, President Woodrow Wilson said, "We entered this war because violations of right had occurred which touched us to the quick and made the life of our own people impossible unless they were corrected, and the world was secure once and for all against their recurrence." The war was finally won that year, and President Wilson went to Paris to negotiate the terms of Germany's capitulation after the conflict had concluded.

80. Who was President during the Great Depression and World War II?

Right answer: (Franklin) Roosevelt

Explanation: From 1933 until his death in 1945, Franklin Delano Roosevelt served as President of the United States of America. He won the presidency amid the Great Depression, which was a time of severe economic hardship that began following the fall of the stock market in 1929. The phrase "the New Deal" was used to refer to his plan for dealing with the problem. It included measures to generate employment, give benefits and financial security to employees around the nation, and provide financial stability for workers. In 1935, he was in charge of establishing what would become the Social Security Administration (SSA). Following the Japanese assault on Pearl Harbor in December 1941, President Roosevelt led the United States into World War II. During a period of enormous difficulty, he instilled a feeling of optimism and fortitude across the nation. Roosevelt won the presidency four times. 1945 marked the beginning of the first year of his fourth term as President when he passed away. Throughout her life, his wife Eleanor Roosevelt was a prominent figure in the fight for civil and political rights.

81. Who did the United States fight in World War II?

Right answer: Germany, Japan, and Italy

Explanation: On December 7, 1941, the Japanese launched an assault on the United States naval bases located at Pearl Harbor, Hawaii. The next day, in his capacity as commander in chief of the armed forces, President Franklin D. Roosevelt requested and received a formal declaration of war from Congress. After this, Japan's allies in the Axis, Italy and Germany, formally declared war on the United States of America. The enemies that the Allies faced were the Nazis of Germany, the Fascists of Italy, and the military empire of Japan. Battles were fought all over the globe, including in Europe, Africa, Asia, and the Pacific Ocean. This war was really a global conflict.

82. Before he was President, Eisenhower was a general. What war was he in?

Right answer: World War II

Explanation: Dwight D. Eisenhower was a major general in the United States Army during World War II. In 1953, he was elected as the 34th President of the United States of America. On June 6, 1944, while serving as the overall commander of the Allied forces in Europe and as commander of the United States troops, he successfully commanded the invasion of Normandy, France, on D-Day. In the year 1952, he took his retirement from active duty in the armed forces. Later in same year, he won the election to become the President of the United States. As president, he was responsible for the creation of the interstate highway system, as well as the Department of Health, Education, and Welfare in 1953, which is now known as the Department of Health and Human Services. He oversaw bringing an end to the Korean War. In 1961, Eisenhower left the White House after having served as president for a total of two terms.

83. During the Cold War, what was the main concern of the United States?

Right answer: Communism

Explanation: During the time of the Cold War, the United States' primary focus was on preventing the growth of communism. The Soviet Union, also known as the Union of Soviet Socialist Republics (USSR), was a formidable country that adhered to the tenets of communism in its daily operations. The United States of

America and its allies believed that maintaining individual rights and freedoms could be accomplished most effectively by maintaining democratic governments and capitalist economies. The United States of America and its allies were concerned about the spread of communism to nations that were not a part of the Soviet Union. The Cold War was a protracted conflict that started not long after the conclusion of World War II and continued for more than four decades. The collapse of the Berlin Wall in 1989, the reunification of East and West Germany in 1990, and the disintegration of the Soviet Union in 1991 were the events that brought about its conclusion.

84. Which movement attempted to put an end to racial discrimination?
Right answer: Civil Rights Movement

Explanation: The Supreme Court's decision in 1954 that it was illegal to maintain racial segregation in public schools in the United States marked the beginning of the modern civil rights movement in that country. The abolition of racial discrimination against African Americans and the attainment of full and equal rights for people of all races in the United States were the primary objectives of the civil rights movement. People gathered to demand social change via the use of nonviolent tactics such as sit-ins, marches, and boycotts of public transportation. As a direct consequence of this, the United States Congress approved the Civil Rights Act of 1964 as well as the Voting Rights Act of 1965. Segregation in public facilities as well as racial discrimination in employment and educational institutions were both declared unlawful by the Civil Rights Act. African Americans, women, and other individuals are protected from discrimination thanks to the legislation. Literacy tests and other additional conditions that were imposed on African Americans to prevent them from registering to vote were made illegal by the Voting Rights Act.

85. What were the accomplishments and contributions of Martin Luther King, Jr.?
Correct answers (choose one):
- Fought for civil rights
- Worked for equality for all Americans

Explanation: Martin Luther King Jr. was a preacher in the Baptist church and a prominent civil rights activist. He exerted a lot of effort to create the United States of America a more just, tolerant, and equitable country. Throughout the 1950s and 1960s, he was the most influential leader of the civil rights movement. As a direct result of this movement, civil rights legislation was enacted to ensure the protection of voting rights and put an end to racial segregation. King was a firm believer in the principles articulated in the Declaration of Independence, including the notion that every American citizen is entitled to the nation's guarantee of equality and justice. In 1963, Martin Luther King Jr. gave his now-famous "I Have a Dream" speech, in which he envisioned an America in which people of all races coexisted equally with one another. When he was awarded the Nobel Peace Prize in 1964 for his involvement in the civil rights movement, he had just turned 35 years old. On April 4, 1968, Martin Luther King Jr. was assassinated.

86. What significant occurrence took place in the United States on September 11, 2001?
Right answer: Terrorists attacked the United States.

Explanation: On the morning of September 11, 2001, terrorists belonging to the Al-Qaeda network of Islamic extremists took control of four aircraft as they were taking off from airports in the United States. Both Twin Towers of the World Trade Center in New York City were destroyed when two of the aircraft collided with the towers during the terrorist attack. There was a collision between one of the aircraft and the Pentagon in Arlington, Virginia. The fourth aircraft, which had been directed for Washington, District of Columbia, ultimately went down in a field in Pennsylvania. These assaults resulted in the deaths of over 3,000 persons, the vast majority of whom were civilians. This was the deadliest assault ever carried out on American soil in the annals of our nation's history.

87. Name one Native American tribe in the United States.
Correct answers (choose one):

- Cherokee
- Navajo
- Sioux
- Chippewa
- Choctaw
- Pueblo
- Apache
- Iroquois
- Creek
- Blackfeet
- Seminole
- Cheyenne
- Arawak
- Shawnee
- Mohegan
- Huron
- Oneida
- Lakota
- Crow
- Teton
- Hopi
- Inuit

Explanation: Before the arrival of European immigrants in North America, Native Americans had already been living there for thousands of years. There are now around 500 indigenous communities in the United States that have been granted federal recognition. Every group or tribe has its own political and social structure. The cultures of the many Native American tribes are distinct from one another, with each tribe having its own distinct set of languages, beliefs, tales, songs, and meals. Earlier in their history, several tribes constructed communities and began farming the land to provide food for themselves. To hunt and collect food and resources, members of other tribes regularly relocated their communities. To relocate tribes to reservations, the federal government sometimes forced them from their homes and other times negotiated and signed treaties with those tribes. These reservations have been acknowledged as independent states inside the United States.

Integrated Civics

A: Geography
88. Provide the name of one of the two longest rivers in the United States.

Correct answers (choose one):

- Mississippi (River)
- Missouri (River)

Explanation: The Mississippi River is one of the longest rivers in the United States. It traverses ten different states in the United States. Before Europeans arrived in the Americas, indigenous people of the region relied on the Mississippi River as a source of commerce, food, and water. It is referred to as the "Father of Waters" by some. Today, the Mississippi River serves as both a significant transportation corridor and a primary supply of drinking water for millions of people along its length. Additionally, the Missouri River is one of the rivers in the United States that is the longest. It's a little-known fact, but the Missouri River is longer than the Mississippi. Its headwaters are in Montana, and it ultimately discharges into the Mississippi River. Jolliet and Marquette, two French explorers, are credited with being the first Europeans to locate the Missouri River in the year 1673. It is known as "Big Muddy" because of the enormous amount of silt it contains.

89. What ocean is on the West Coast of the U.S.?
Right answer: Pacific Ocean

Explanation: Along the western coast of the United States is where you'll find the Pacific Ocean. It is the world's biggest ocean, and it takes up about a third of the surface area of our planet. The Pacific Ocean is significant to the economy of the United States due to the abundance of natural resources that can be found there, such as fish. It wasn't until the 16th century that Europeans obtained their first knowledge of the Pacific Ocean. When he crossed the Isthmus of Panama in 1514, the Spanish explorer Vasco Nez de Balboa became the first European to see the ocean. After some time had passed, Ferdinand Magellan continued his voyage around the world by sailing across the Pacific Ocean in quest of spices. "Pacific" implies "peaceful". Magellan christened the Pacific Ocean with the moniker "peaceful sea" because he encountered no violent weather on his voyage from Spain to the spice world. The states of Alaska, Washington, Oregon, California, and Hawaii are the ones that form the United States' coastline along the Pacific Ocean.

90. Which Ocean is located along the East Coast of the United States?
Right answer: Atlantic Ocean

Explanation: The East Coast of the United States is where you will find the Atlantic Ocean. The legendary titan Atlas of Greek mythology inspired the naming of this water body. It is the world's second-largest ocean after the Pacific. The Atlantic Ocean serves as a significant transportation corridor for ships. It sees more traffic than any other body of water on the planet. The Atlantic Ocean is another location where a great deal of natural resources may be found. The North American and European continents broke apart many millions of years ago, which resulted in the formation of the Atlantic Ocean. The oceans take up around twenty percent of the surface area of the earth. The Mid-Atlantic Ridge is a massive underwater mountain range that runs the length of the Atlantic Ocean and is a source of volcanic activity. This mountain range may be found in the middle of the ocean. The following states in the United States have a coastline on the Atlantic Ocean: Connecticut, Delaware, Florida, Georgia, Maine, Maryland, Massachusetts, New Hampshire, New Jersey, New York, North Carolina, Rhode Island, and South Carolina.

91. Name one U.S. territory
Correct answers (choose one):

- Puerto Rico
- U.S. Virgin Islands
- American Samoa
- Northern Mariana Islands

- Guam

Explanation: American Samoa, Guam, the Northern Mariana Islands, Puerto Rico, and the United States Virgin Islands are the five principal territories that make up the United States of America. A portion of land that is under the jurisdiction of the United States government but has some degree of autonomy on its own is known as a territory of the United States. Even though they are not states, the territories of the United States do have a voice in Congress. It is permissible for each area to send one representative to serve in the House of Representatives. People who live in American Samoa are regarded to be citizens of the United States, whereas residents of the other four territories are nationals of the United States. People who live in the territories have the right to vote in the primaries for President, but they are not allowed to vote in the general election for President.

92. Name one state that borders Canada
Correct answers (choose one):
- Maine
- New Hampshire
- Vermont
- New York
- Pennsylvania
- Ohio
- Michigan
- Minnesota
- North Dakota
- Montana
- Idaho
- Washington
- Alaska

Explanation: More than 5,000 miles separate the easternmost state of Maine from the westernmost state of Alaska along the length of the northern frontier of the United States. There are 13 states that are directly next to Canada's border. Following the conclusion of the American Revolutionary War, an official border between the United States and Canada was defined by the Treaty of Paris in 1783. Since then, there have been disagreements over territory, but those disagreements have been settled via the use of treaties. The responsibility for the upkeep of the line falls on the shoulders of the International Line Commission, which is led by a pair of commissioners, one from the United States and one from Canada.

93. Name one state that borders Mexico
Correct answers (choose one):
- Arizona
- New Mexico
- California
- Texas

Explanation: About 1,900 miles long, the border that separates the United States of America and Mexico runs along four different states in the United States: Arizona, California, New Mexico, and Texas. Following the conclusion of the Mexican-American War and the completion of the Gadsden Purchase in 1853, the

United States demarcated its boundary with Mexico. The United States was able to acquire more territory for the expansion of the southern railroad because of the Gadsden Purchase. The United States of America spent $10 million to acquire this piece of property. The Gadsden Purchase resulted in the territory that is today the states of Arizona and New Mexico. The border between the United States and Mexico is often ranked as one of the busiest international frontiers in the world.

94. What is the capital of the United States?
Right answer: Washington, D.C.

Explanation: In the year 1789, when the Constitution was ratified and our country was officially founded, New York City served as the nation's capital. As quickly as possible, Congress started debating where the permanent capital should be located. There was a heated debate going on in Congress between members of northern states and representatives of southern states. Each faction advocated for the location of the capital to be inside its own territory. In accordance with the terms of the Compromise of 1790, the nation's capital would be situated in what was then the southern region. In exchange, the North was absolved of the debt that resulted from its participation in the Revolutionary War. Between the states of Maryland and Virginia, along the Potomac River, is where George Washington decided to build the nation's capital. As a result of the agreement, Philadelphia, in the state of Pennsylvania, was selected to serve as the nation's capital during the interim. After a period of 10 years, in the year 1800, the capital was relocated to its present site of Washington, District of Columbia.

95. Where is the Statue of Liberty?
Correct answers (choose one):
- New York Harbor
- Liberty Island
- New Jersey,
- Near New York City
- On the Hudson River

Explanation: The Statue of Liberty may be found on Liberty Island, a small island in the New York Port that covers around 12 acres. As a token of their friendship, the French government presented the United States with the monument. Frederic-Auguste Bartholdi, a French artist, was the one who created the statue. It depicts a lady breaking free from the shackles of oppression while carrying a torch, which stands for freedom. On October 28, 1886, exactly 110 years after the writing of the Declaration of Independence, the Statue of Liberty was finally given its proper dedication. The gift was received on behalf of the people of the United States by President Grover Cleveland. The Statue of Liberty is an internationally recognized emblem not just of the United States but also of democracy and freedom. Because of its proximity to Ellis Island, which served as the primary port of entry for a significant number of immigrants throughout the many waves of immigration, the Statue of Liberty has come to be seen as a symbol of immigration. As they entered New York Harbor, newly arrived immigrants were greeted with a view of the Statue of Liberty for the first time.

B: Symbols

96. What is the reason behind the presence of 13 stripes on the flag?
Correct answers (choose one):
- Because the stripes represent the original colonies
- Because there were 13 original colonies

Explanation: Because there were once thirteen states that comprised the United States, our flag has thirteen horizontal stripes. "The Stars and Stripes" is the common name for the American flag. Only 13 stripes appeared on the flag of the United States during the first 18 years after that nation achieved its independence. In 1794, Kentucky and Vermont became members of the United States, which prompted the addition of two more stripes to the flag. The United States Congress made the decision in 1818 that the number of stripes on the flag should remain constant at 13. This would be a fitting tribute to the founding states, all of which had been colonies of Great Britain before the United States' declaration of independence.

97. What is the significance of having 50 stars on the flag?
Correct answers (choose one):
- Because each star represents a state
- Because there are 50 states
- Because there is one star for each state

Explanation: Each of the 50 states is represented with a star on the flag. Because of this, the number of stars has increased from 13 to 50 throughout the course of so many years. In 1959, when Hawaii became the 50th state of the United States, the total number of stars reached its maximum of fifty. The First Flag Act was enacted in 1777 by the Second Continental Congress. It said, "Resolved, That the flag of the United States be made of thirteen stripes, alternate red and white; that the union be thirteen stars, white in a blue field, representing a new Constellation." The stripes were to be red and white, and the stars were to be white.

98. What is the name of the national anthem?
Right answer: The Star-Spangled Banner

Explanation: The United States was invaded by forces from the United Kingdom during the War of 1812. On the night of September 13, 1814, British warships launched an attack on Fort McHenry by dropping bombs on the fort. This fort guarded the entrance of Baltimore, Maryland. Francis Scott Key, an American, saw the bombardment and became certain that the fort would be destroyed as a result. Key turned his attention toward the fort as the sun began to rise the next morning. He saw that the flag that had been raised atop the stronghold was still flying. This made it clear to him that the British had not been successful in their battle against the Americans. After that, Key started writing the lines of a poem that he would later name "Defense of Fort M'Henry." The poem was later adapted into the national anthem known as "The Star-Spangled Banner." In 1931, the statute that established "The Star-Spangled Banner" as the nation's official "National Anthem" was enacted by Congress.

The Star-Spangled Banner:
Oh, say, can you see, by the dawn's early light,
What so proudly we hailed at the twilight's last gleaming?
Whose broad stripes and bright stars, thro' the perilous fight;
O'er the ramparts we watched, were so gallantly streaming.
And the rockets' red glare, the bombs bursting in air,
Gave proof through the night that our flag was still there.
Oh, say, does that star-spangled banner yet wave
O'er the land of the free and the home of the brave?

C: Holidays
99. When do we celebrate Independence Day?
Right answer: July 4

Explanation: The adoption of the Declaration of Independence is commemorated as the occasion for the annual holiday known as Independence Day in the United States. This holiday is observed on July 4th. John Adams wrote to his wife shortly after signing the Declaration of Independence, "I am apt to believe that it will be celebrated, by succeeding Generations, as the great anniversary Festival." Thomas Jefferson's Declaration of Independence provided an explanation for the reasons for the colonies' decision to declare their independence from Great Britain. Parades, fireworks, patriotic music, and readings from the Declaration of Independence are just few of the ways that the Fourth of July is celebrated as the birthday of the United States of America by its citizens.

100. Name two national U.S. holidays
Correct answers (choose two):
- New Year's Day
- Martin Luther King, Jr. Day
- Presidents' Day
- Memorial Day
- Independence Day
- Labor Day
- Columbus Day
- Veterans Day
- Thanksgiving
- Christmas

Explanation: Many people in the country observe days that are designated as national or federal holidays. Many significant personalities or events in our American history are honored on these holidays. Only federal institutions and residents of the District of Columbia are required to observe these holidays as "national" in accordance with the law. Most of the time, government buildings and offices are closed on these days. It is up to the individual states to determine whether to observe the holiday. On these days, businesses, schools, and other commercial enterprises have the option of remaining open or closing their doors. Since 1971, New Year's Day, Independence Day, Veterans Day, Thanksgiving, and Christmas are the only holidays that are not commemorated on Mondays as part of the federal holiday calendar.

4.1.1 Principles Of American Democracy

The principles of American democracy serve as the bedrock of the nation's political system. They embody the core values and ideals upon which the United States was founded and continue to guide its governance and society. As part of the civic education test for naturalization, applicants are evaluated on their knowledge and understanding of these principles. In this section, we will explore various questions, along with their corresponding answers and quick explanations, that pertain to the principles of American democracy.

Question: What is the rule of law?

Answer: The rule of law is the principle that all individuals and institutions are subject to and accountable to the law. No one is above the law.

Quick Explanation: The rule of law is a fundamental concept in American democracy. It ensures that laws apply equally to all individuals, including government officials, and serves as a safeguard against arbitrary exercise of power. Upholding the rule of law is essential for maintaining justice, order, and fairness within society.

Question: What is the significance of the First Amendment?

Answer: The First Amendment guarantees several fundamental freedoms, including freedom of speech, religion, press, assembly, and the right to petition the government for grievances.

Quick Explanation: The First Amendment is a cornerstone of American democracy, protecting the rights of individuals to express their opinions freely, practice any religion of their choice, publish and access diverse sources of information, peacefully assemble, and petition the government to address grievances. These freedoms foster a vibrant exchange of ideas, ensure religious liberty, and promote an informed citizenry.

Question: What does "separation of powers" mean?

Answer: Separation of powers refers to the division of government authority among three branches - the executive, legislative, and judicial - each with distinct powers and responsibilities.

Quick Explanation: The concept of separation of powers is central to the U.S. Constitution and aims to prevent the concentration of power in any single branch. The executive branch enforces laws, the legislative branch makes laws, and the judicial branch interprets laws. This system of checks and balances ensures accountability, prevents abuse of power, and safeguards individual rights.

Question: What is federalism?

Answer: Federalism is the system of government in which power is divided between a central authority, the federal government, and individual state governments.

Quick Explanation: Federalism strikes a balance between national unity and regional autonomy. The federal government handles national matters such as defense and foreign policy, while state governments address local concerns like education and public safety. Federalism fosters collaboration, accommodates diverse needs, and allows states to experiment with policies within constitutional boundaries.

Question: What is the importance of civic participation?

Answer: Civic participation refers to the active involvement of citizens in their communities and the democratic process, including voting, volunteering, and engaging in public discourse.

Quick Explanation: Civic participation is vital to the functioning of a healthy democracy. When citizens actively engage in their communities and exercise their rights and responsibilities, they contribute to the decision-making processes and help shape public policies. By voting in elections, participating in community initiatives, and expressing their views, individuals play an active role in shaping the direction of their society.

Question: What is the significance of the principle of equality?

Answer: The principle of equality declares that every person should receive equitable and impartial treatment under the law, regardless of race, gender, religion, or any other protected attributes.

Quick Explanation: Equality is a fundamental value that underpins American democracy. It guarantees that all individuals have the same rights, opportunities, and protections, fostering a society that values diversity, inclusivity, and social justice. Upholding equality helps to eliminate discrimination and ensure equal access to education, employment, and the pursuit of happiness.

Question: What is the role of the citizen in a democracy?

Answer: The role of the citizen in a democracy is to participate actively in the democratic process, uphold the laws, and contribute to the betterment of society.

Quick Explanation: Citizens play a crucial role in a democracy by exercising their rights and fulfilling their responsibilities. This includes voting in elections, staying informed about current issues, serving on juries, obeying laws, paying taxes, and actively engaging in their communities. Citizen participation strengthens democracy, promotes social cohesion, and helps maintain the welfare of the nation.

Question: What is the importance of the principle of checks and balances?

Answer: The principle of checks and balances ensures that no single branch of government becomes too powerful by providing mechanisms for each branch to limit the actions of the other branches.

Quick Explanation: Checks and balances are crucial in preventing the abuse of power and maintaining a system of accountability. The executive, legislative, and judicial branches of government play separate roles and hold distinct powers. They serve as checks on each other's authority. For example, the President can reject legislation passed by Congress by exercising veto power, but Congress can override the veto with a two-thirds majority vote. This system promotes collaboration, prevents the concentration of power, and safeguards the rights and interests of the people.

Question: What is the significance of the principle of individual rights?

Answer: The principle of individual rights protects the fundamental liberties and freedoms of every person, such as freedom of speech, religion, and the right to a fair trial.

Quick Explanation: Individual rights are essential in a democratic society as they safeguard the autonomy and dignity of individuals. These rights, enshrined in the U.S. Constitution and the Bill of Rights, protect citizens from undue government interference and ensure their ability to express themselves, practice their beliefs, and seek justice. Recognizing and respecting individual rights is vital for promoting a just and inclusive society that values the inherent worth and autonomy of every person.

Question: What is the significance of the principle of popular sovereignty?

Answer: Popular sovereignty asserts that the ultimate source of political power rests with the people, who exercise their power through voting and participating in the democratic process.

Quick Explanation: Popular sovereignty is a fundamental principle of American democracy, emphasizing that the government derives its authority from the consent of the governed. In a democratic system, the people have the power to elect their representatives, shape public policies through their votes, and hold their elected officials accountable. This principle ensures that the government remains responsive to the will of the people and serves their best interests.

Understanding and appreciating these principles of American democracy is essential for individuals seeking to become U.S. citizens. By demonstrating their knowledge of these principles and their commitment to upholding democratic values, applicants show their readiness to embrace the rights, responsibilities, and privileges that come with citizenship. Moreover, a well-informed citizenry that understands the principles upon which the nation was built is crucial for the continued strength and vitality of American democracy.

4.1.2 The Governance System

The governance system of the United States is built upon a foundation of democratic principles and structures that ensure the smooth functioning of the government. Understanding how the governance system works is crucial for individuals seeking to become U.S. citizens, as it enables them to actively participate in the democratic process and contribute to the nation's progress. In this section, we will explore a series of questions, along with their answers and quick explanations, to provide a comprehensive understanding of the governance system in the United States.

Question: What is the structure of the U.S. government?

Answer: The U.S. government is structured as a federal system with three branches: the executive, legislative, and judicial branches.

Quick Explanation: The federal system divides power between the national government and state governments. The executive branch, led by the President, enforces laws; the legislative branch, consisting of Congress, makes laws; and the judicial branch, headed by the Supreme Court, interprets laws. This separation of powers ensures a system of checks and balances to prevent the concentration of authority in any one branch.

Question: What are the powers of the executive branch?

Answer: The executive branch is responsible for executing and enforcing laws, commanding the military, conducting foreign relations, and proposing legislation.

Quick Explanation: The executive branch, headed by the President, has the authority to implement laws passed by Congress and make executive decisions. The President also serves as the Commander-in-Chief of the military and negotiates treaties with foreign nations and proposes legislation to Congress. The executive branch plays a vital role in the day-to-day operations of the government and is responsible for implementing policies that impact the nation and its citizens.

Question: What is the role of Congress?

Answer: Congress, consisting of the House of Representatives and the Senate, is responsible for making laws, representing the interests of the people, and overseeing the federal government.

Quick Explanation: Congress is the legislative branch of the U.S. government and has the power to make laws. The House of Representatives, with its members based on each state's population, and the Senate, with two members from each state, work together to pass legislation that affects the nation. Congress also plays a vital role in representing the interests of the people, conducting oversight of the executive branch, and shaping public policy.

Question: What is the role of the judicial branch?

Answer: The judicial branch is responsible for interpreting laws, resolving disputes, and upholding the Constitution.

Quick Explanation: The judicial branch, led by the Supreme Court, has the authority to interpret the meaning and application of laws. It ensures that laws are consistent with the Constitution and resolves disputes through the legal system. The Supreme Court has the final say on matters of constitutional interpretation and plays a crucial role in safeguarding individual rights and maintaining the balance of power within the government.

Question: How are federal judges appointed?

Answer: Federal judges, including Supreme Court justices, are nominated by the President and confirmed by the Senate.

Quick Explanation: The appointment of federal judges, including Supreme Court justices, is a shared responsibility between the President and the Senate. The President nominates candidates for federal judgeships, and the Senate reviews the nominations and conducts confirmation hearings. Once confirmed, federal judges serve lifetime appointments, ensuring their independence and impartiality in interpreting and applying the law.

Question: What is the importance of the Constitution?

Answer: The Constitution is the supreme law of the land and establishes the framework for the U.S. government, guarantees fundamental rights, and outlines the powers and limitations of each branch of government.

Quick Explanation: The Constitution is the foundation of the U.S. governance system, providing the framework for the organization and functioning of the government. It establishes the separation of powers, outlines the rights and freedoms of individuals, and sets limits on the authority of the government. The Constitution is a living document that adapts to the changing needs of society through amendments and interpretations by the judiciary.

Question: How can citizens participate in the governance system?

Answer: Citizens can participate in the governance system by voting, engaging in peaceful protests, serving on juries, running for public office, and staying informed about current issues.

Quick Explanation: Active citizen participation is crucial for a thriving democracy. Citizens can exercise their right to vote in elections to choose their representatives, voice their opinions through peaceful protests, serve on juries to ensure fair trials, and even run for public office. Staying informed about current issues and engaging in constructive dialogue with elected officials and fellow citizens are also essential for effective participation in the governance system.

Question: What is the significance of federalism in the U.S. governance system?

Answer: Federalism divides power between the national government and state governments, allowing for shared and independent decision-making on various issues.

Quick Explanation: Federalism ensures a balance of power between the national government and state governments. It allows the national government to address matters of national concern, such as defense and foreign policy, while granting states the authority to govern within their own jurisdictions. This system fosters cooperation and collaboration between different levels of government and allows for tailored governance based on local needs and preferences.

Question: How can the governance system be improved?

Answer: The governance system can be improved through active citizen engagement, transparent and accountable governance practices, and ongoing dialogue between elected officials and the public.

Quick Explanation: Continuous improvement of the governance system requires the active involvement of citizens. This includes holding elected officials accountable, advocating for reforms, and participating in decision-making processes. Transparent and accountable governance practices, such as open access to information and ethical conduct by public officials, are essential for building trust and ensuring effective governance. Additionally, fostering an environment of open dialogue and collaboration between elected officials and the public can lead to innovative solutions and inclusive decision-making processes.

Question: What is the role of political parties in the governance system?

Answer: Political parties play a significant role in the governance system by shaping public policy, mobilizing voters, and providing a platform for political candidates to express their ideologies and proposals.

Quick Explanation: Political parties are organizations that represent specific political ideologies and interests. They serve as a means for individuals to collectively promote their shared values and ideas. Political parties play a crucial role in the governance system by formulating policy agendas, advocating for legislative changes, and influencing public opinion. They serve as a platform for candidates to present their political platforms and seek public support through elections. Political parties also contribute to the functioning of the legislative branch by organizing members and facilitating the passage of legislation aligned with their party's goals. Political parties serve as a vital link between citizens and the government, shaping the political landscape and facilitating the democratic process.

4.1.3 Rights and Duties

Rights and duties are fundamental aspects of citizenship in any democratic society. They define the relationship between individuals and the government, outlining the freedoms and responsibilities that citizens possess. Understanding these rights and duties is essential for active citizenship and informed participation in the governance system. In this section, we will explore ten questions related to rights and duties, along with their answers and quick explanations.

Question: What are civil rights?

Answer: Civil rights are the fundamental rights and freedoms that protect individuals from discrimination and ensure equal treatment under the law.

Quick Explanation: Civil rights encompass the basic rights and freedoms guaranteed to all citizens, such as the right to life, liberty, and the pursuit of happiness. These rights encompass freedom of speech, religion, and assembly, along with the right to vote, a fair trial, and protection against discrimination based on factors such as race, gender, or ethnicity. Civil rights are crucial for upholding individual liberties and promoting a just and inclusive society.

Question: What is the significance of the First Amendment?

Answer: The First Amendment protects freedom of speech, religion, the press, peaceful assembly, and the right to petition the government.

Quick Explanation: The First Amendment of the United States Constitution is of paramount importance as it guarantees several fundamental freedoms. It safeguards the right to express one's opinions, practice any religion, and disseminate information through the press. Additionally, it protects the right to peacefully assemble and petition the government for grievances, ensuring that citizens can voice their concerns and engage in open dialogue without fear of reprisal.

Question: What are the responsibilities of citizens in a democracy?

Answer: The responsibilities of citizens in a democracy include voting, staying informed, participating in civic activities, obeying laws, and respecting the rights of others.

Quick Explanation: Active citizen participation is essential for the functioning of a healthy democracy. Citizens have a responsibility to exercise their right to vote, as it allows them to influence the selection of their representatives and shape the policies of their government. Staying informed about current events, engaging in civic activities, obeying laws, and respecting the rights and opinions of others are all important aspects of responsible citizenship.

Question: What is the right to due process?

Answer: The right to due process ensures that individuals are treated fairly and can defend themselves in legal proceedings.

Quick Explanation: The right to due process is a fundamental legal principle that guarantees individuals fair and impartial treatment under the law. This ensures that no individual can be deprived of life, liberty, or property without proper legal procedures and protections. These rights encompass the right to a fair trial, the presumption of innocence, the right to legal representation, and the ability to present evidence and contest allegations.

Question: What is the significance of the Fourteenth Amendment?

Answer: The Fourteenth Amendment guarantees equal protection under the law and prohibits states from denying individuals their rights without due process.

Quick Explanation: The Fourteenth Amendment is a pivotal constitutional provision that affirms equal protection of the law for all citizens. It prohibits states from denying individuals their basic rights and liberties without following proper legal procedures. This amendment has been instrumental in advancing civil rights and combating discrimination based on race, gender, and other protected characteristics. It ensures that all individuals are treated equally and enjoy the same rights and opportunities.

Question: What are the rights and responsibilities of the press?

Answer: The rights of freedom of the press include gathering and disseminating information without censorship or government interference. The responsibilities of the press include reporting accurately, maintaining journalistic ethics, and serving as a watchdog of government.

Quick Explanation: Freedom of the press is essential for a democratic society as it enables journalists to investigate and report on matters of public interest without censorship or undue influence. It ensures the free flow of information, holds the government accountable, and facilitates public discourse. However, with these rights come responsibilities. Journalists have a duty to report accurately, adhere to professional, ethical standards, verify information, and provide balanced and unbiased coverage.

Question: What is the significance of the right to bear arms?

Answer: The right to bear arms, as outlined in the Second Amendment, allows individuals to possess firearms for self-defense and other lawful purposes.

Quick Explanation: The Second Amendment of the United States Constitution enshrines the right of individuals to possess firearms. It recognizes the importance of self-defense and the need for citizens to protect themselves, their families, and their property. However, the right to bear arms is subject to reasonable regulation and does not grant unlimited access to firearms. It is a topic of ongoing debate, and lawmakers continually seek to strike a balance between ensuring public safety and preserving individual rights.

Question: What are the rights of individuals accused of a crime?

Answer: Individuals accused of a crime are entitled to certain rights, including the right to remain silent, the right to legal representation, the right to a fair trial, and the presumption of innocence until proven guilty.

Quick Explanation: The rights of individuals accused of a crime are crucial to safeguarding the principles of justice and fairness. These rights include the right to remain silent to avoid self-incrimination, the right to legal representation, the right to a fair trial by an impartial jury, and the presumption of innocence until proven guilty. These protections ensure that individuals are treated fairly throughout the criminal justice process and that their rights are upheld.

Question: What is the significance of the Nineteenth Amendment?

Answer: The Nineteenth Amendment granted women the right to vote, ensuring gender equality in the electoral process.

Quick Explanation: The Nineteenth Amendment, ratified in 1920, was a landmark achievement in the fight for women's suffrage. It granted women the right to vote, a crucial step toward achieving gender equality in the democratic process. This amendment recognized the fundamental principle that all citizens, regardless of gender, should have the right to participate in shaping the government and electing their representatives.

Question: What are the rights and responsibilities of a naturalized citizen?

Answer: Naturalized citizens enjoy the same rights and protections as native-born citizens, including the right to vote and the right to free speech. They also have the responsibility to uphold the laws, support the Constitution, and serve on juries when called upon.

Quick Explanation: Naturalized citizens have gone through the process of becoming U.S. citizens and, as such, enjoy the same rights and protections as those who are native-born. They have the right to vote in elections, express their opinions freely, and enjoy the freedoms guaranteed by the Constitution. Alongside these rights, naturalized citizens also have responsibilities. They are expected to uphold the country's laws , support the Constitution, and fulfill their civic duty by serving on juries when called upon. These responsibilities ensure that naturalized citizens actively participate in the democratic process and contribute to the nation's well-being.

Understanding rights and duties is vital for every citizen. By familiarizing themselves with these fundamental principles, individuals can fully engage in their communities, contribute to the democratic process, and protect the rights and freedoms that underpin a just and inclusive society.

4.1.4 History of the United States - The Colonial Period and Independence

The colonial period and the struggle for independence form a significant chapter in the history of the United States. This era marked the early settlement of the American colonies, the growth of colonial society, and the eventual quest for independence from British rule. In this section, we will explore a series of questions related to the colonial period and the fight for independence, providing answers and quick explanations for each.

Question: When did the first permanent English settlement in North America occur?

Answer: The first permanent English settlement in North America was founded in 1607 with the establishment of Jamestown in Virginia.

Quick Explanation: Jamestown, established by the Virginia Company, was the first successful English settlement in the New World. It served as a foothold for further English colonization efforts and paved the way for the establishment of future colonies in North America.

Question: What was the Mayflower Compact?

Answer: The Mayflower Compact was a governing document created by the Pilgrims aboard the Mayflower in 1620, establishing self-government and majority rule in the Plymouth colony.

Quick Explanation: The Mayflower Compact was a significant step in developing democratic principles in the American colonies. It represented an agreement among the Pilgrims to establish a form of self-government, ensuring that decisions would be made through majority rule and for the general good of the colony.

Question: What was the significance of establishing the Massachusetts Bay Colony in 1630?

Answer: The establishment of the Massachusetts Bay Colony in 1630 marked the beginning of a large-scale migration of Puritans seeking religious freedom, contributing to the growth of English colonies in North America.

Quick Explanation: The Massachusetts Bay Colony was established by a group of Puritans known as the Massachusetts Bay Company. Their migration to North America in search of religious freedom played a crucial role in shaping the religious, social, and political landscape of the New England colonies.

Question: What were the causes of the French and Indian War?

Answer: The French and Indian War, fought from 1754 to 1763, was primarily caused by conflicts over territorial expansion between the French and British in North America.

Quick Explanation: The French and Indian War was part of a larger global conflict known as the Seven Years' War. It was primarily fought between the British and French, along with their respective Native American allies. The war resulted from tensions over territorial claims, control of trade routes, and competition for resources in the Ohio River Valley.

Question: What was the significance of the Proclamation of 1763?

Answer: The Proclamation of 1763 was issued by the British government and aimed to stabilize relations with Native American tribes by restricting colonial settlement west of the Appalachian Mountains.

Quick Explanation: The Proclamation of 1763 sought to ease tensions with Native American tribes following the French and Indian War. It prohibited colonial settlement west of the Appalachian Mountains, which led to resentment among some colonists who desired to expand into the newly acquired territories.

Question: What were the Intolerable Acts, and how did they impact the American colonies?

Answer: The Intolerable Acts were a series of punitive measures imposed by the British Parliament in response to the Boston Tea Party. They limited self-governance, restricted colonial trade, and increased British military presence in the colonies.

Quick Explanation: The Intolerable Acts were enacted as a direct response to the Boston Tea Party, a colonial protest against British taxation. These acts included the closure of the Boston Harbor, the suspension of self-governance in Massachusetts, and the quartering of British troops in private homes. They further fueled the growing discontent among colonists and contributed to the push for independence.

Question: What was the significance of the Declaration of Independence?

Answer: The Declaration of Independence, adopted on July 4, 1776, proclaimed the thirteen American colonies as independent states, severing ties with British rule and laying the foundation for the United States of America.

Quick Explanation: The Declaration of Independence, primarily drafted by Thomas Jefferson, declared the colonies' intent to break away from British rule and established the fundamental principles of individual rights, equality, and government by consent. It became a rallying cry for the American Revolution and remained one of the most important documents in American history.

Question: Who were the Founding Fathers, and what role did they play in shaping the United States?

Answer: The Founding Fathers were influential leaders who participated in the American Revolution, drafted the U.S. Constitution, and established the principles and institutions of the new nation.

Quick Explanation: The Founding Fathers include notable figures such as George Washington, Thomas Jefferson, Benjamin Franklin, James Madison, Alexander Hamilton, and John Adams, among others. They played a crucial role in shaping the United States, contributing to the establishment of democratic principles, the separation of powers, and the creation of a federal system of government.

Question: What were the Articles of Confederation, and why were they ultimately replaced by the U.S. Constitution?

Answer: The Articles of Confederation served as the first national constitution of the United States, but their weaknesses led to the adoption of the U.S. Constitution. The Articles created a weak central government with limited powers, resulting in difficulties in governing the young nation effectively.

Quick Explanation: The Articles of Confederation, ratified in 1781, established a loose alliance among the thirteen states. However, the Articles proved ineffective in addressing economic, political, and military challenges. This led to the Constitutional Convention in 1787, where delegates drafted the U.S. Constitution, creating a stronger federal government and addressing the shortcomings of the Articles.

Question: What role did the American Revolution play in inspiring other movements for independence around the world?

Answer: The success of the American Revolution in achieving independence from British rule inspired other nations and peoples to fight for their own freedom and independence.

Quick Explanation: The American Revolution served as a beacon of hope for oppressed people around the world. The principles of liberty, self-determination, and resistance to tyranny embodied by the American Revolution inspired subsequent revolutions and movements for independence, including the French Revolution and the struggles for independence in Latin America.

The colonial period and the fight for independence laid the foundation for the birth of the United States as a nation. It was a time of exploration, settlement, political development, and a quest for individual rights and freedoms. Understanding this period in American history is essential to grasp the ideals and values that continue to shape the nation to this day.

4.1.5 US History - The Nineteenth Century

The nineteenth century was a pivotal period in American history, marked by significant social, political, and economic changes. From westward expansion to the Civil War and reconstruction, this era shaped the nation's identity and laid the groundwork for its future development. In this section, we will explore a series of questions, answers, and quick explanations related to the major events and themes of the nineteenth century in American history.

Question: What was the significance of the Louisiana Purchase?

Answer: The Louisiana Purchase, made in 1803, doubled the size of the United States and opened vast western territories for exploration and settlement.

Quick Explanation: The Louisiana Purchase was a landmark event during President Thomas Jefferson's administration. It involved the acquisition of a vast territory from France, stretching from the Mississippi River to the Rocky Mountains. This acquisition not only provided valuable natural resources but also expanded the nation's borders and paved the way for westward expansion.

Question: What were the causes of the War of 1812?

Answer: The War of 1812 was primarily caused by British maritime restrictions, impressment of American sailors, and conflicts over territorial expansion in North America.

Quick Explanation: The War of 1812 was fought between the United States and Great Britain. The British imposed trade restrictions and often seized American ships and sailors, leading to growing tensions. Additionally, territorial disputes, such as the British support of Native American resistance to American expansion, contributed to the outbreak of the war.

Question: What impact did the Monroe Doctrine have on U.S. foreign policy?

Answer: The Monroe Doctrine, declared in 1823, established the United States as the dominant power in the Western Hemisphere and warned European nations against further colonization or intervention in the Americas.

Quick Explanation: The Monroe Doctrine, named after President James Monroe, asserted the United States' authority in the Western Hemisphere and signaled its opposition to European interference. It became a foundational principle of American foreign policy, shaping relations with Latin American countries and influencing future U.S. actions in the region.

Question: *What factors contributed to the rapid growth of cotton production in the South?*

Answer: The growth of cotton production in the South was primarily fueled by the invention of the cotton gin, the expansion of slavery, and the demand for cotton in the textile industry.

Quick Explanation: Eli Whitney's invention of the cotton gin in 1793 revolutionized cotton production by mechanizing the separation of seeds from cotton fibers. This made cotton cultivation more profitable and led to a significant increase in the demand for enslaved labor. The profitability of cotton production drove the expansion of slavery and shaped the economy and society of the antebellum South.

Question: *What was the significance of the Missouri Compromise of 1820?*

Answer: The Missouri Compromise temporarily resolved the issue of slavery expansion by admitting Missouri as a slave state and Maine as a free state while drawing a line across the Louisiana Territory to determine future slave and free states.

Quick Explanation: As the United States expanded westward, the issue of slavery's expansion into new territories became increasingly contentious. The Missouri Compromise, proposed by Henry Clay, sought to maintain a balance between slave and free states. It demonstrated the ongoing tensions between the North and the South over the issue of slavery and set a precedent for future compromises.

Question: *What were the key causes of the Mexican-American War?*

Answer: The Mexican-American War, fought from 1846 to 1848, was primarily caused by border disputes, the annexation of Texas, and differing visions of westward expansion.

Quick Explanation: The Mexican-American War was triggered by the annexation of Texas by the United States in 1845, which Mexico considered an act of aggression. Border disputes, particularly regarding the Texas-Mexico boundary, further heightened tensions. The concept of "Manifest Destiny," the belief in American expansionism, also played a role in fueling the conflict.

Question: *What were the main goals and outcomes of the abolitionist movement?*

Answer: The abolitionist movement aimed to end slavery in the United States, advocating for the immediate emancipation of enslaved people. Its efforts contributed to the eventual abolition of slavery and the Civil War.

Quick Explanation: Abolitionists, such as Frederick Douglass, Harriet Tubman, and William Lloyd Garrison, campaigned to eradicate slavery based on moral, religious, and humanitarian grounds. Their activism helped raise awareness about the cruelty and injustice of slavery and galvanized support for its abolition. The movement played a significant role in shaping public opinion and ultimately led to the Emancipation Proclamation and the Thirteenth Amendment, which abolished slavery.

Question: *What were the causes and consequences of the Civil War?*

Answer: The Civil War was primarily caused by disagreements over slavery, states' rights, and differing economic and social systems between the North and the South. Its consequences included the preservation of the Union, the end of slavery, and the reshaping of the nation.

Quick Explanation: The Civil War, fought from 1861 to 1865, was a result of deep-rooted divisions between the Northern states, which favored industrialization and opposed slavery, and the Southern states, which relied on slave labor and defended states' rights. The war resulted in the preservation of the Union and the abolition of slavery with the ratification of the Thirteenth Amendment. It also brought about significant changes in the country's political, economic, and social landscape.

Question: What was the purpose and impact of Reconstruction after the Civil War?

Answer: Reconstruction was a period of rebuilding and reuniting the United States after the Civil War. Its goals included integrating former Confederate states back into the Union, granting rights to formerly enslaved individuals, and addressing the social and economic aftermath of the war.

Quick Explanation: Reconstruction aimed to address the challenges of reintegrating the Southern states into the Union and securing civil rights for African Americans. It led to the passage of the Reconstruction Amendments (the Thirteenth, Fourteenth, and Fifteenth Amendments), which abolished slavery, granted equal protection under the law, and ensured voting rights for African-American men. However, Reconstruction was cut short by political opposition and the rise of segregationist policies, limiting its long-term impact.

Question: What were the main causes and effects of westward expansion in the nineteenth century?

Answer: Westward expansion was driven by various factors, including economic opportunities, the belief in Manifest Destiny, and government policies. Its effects included the displacement of Native American tribes, the growth of the nation's economy, and the transformation of the United States into a continental power.

Quick Explanation: Westward expansion involved the movement of settlers and pioneers to the western territories, fueled by the lure of fertile land, the discovery of gold and other natural resources, and the vision of expanding American influence from coast to coast. However, this expansion resulted in the displacement and marginalization of Native American tribes, leading to conflicts and the loss of their lands. It also contributed to the growth of the U.S. economy, the development of infrastructure, and the consolidation of a vast nation.

The nineteenth century in American history was a period of immense transformation, with events and developments that shaped the nation's identity and trajectory. From territorial acquisitions to the abolition of slavery, each question and its explanation provides insights into the key historical events, ideas, and consequences that defined this crucial era. By understanding the history of the nineteenth century, we gain a deeper appreciation for the challenges, triumphs, and complexities that have shaped the United States into the nation it is today.

4.1.6 Modern and Contemporary History and Other Relevant Historical Facts

Studying modern and contemporary history is essential for understanding the events, developments, and significant shifts that have shaped the world we live in today. This period encompasses a range of transformative events, including world wars, political revolutions, social movements, technological advancements, and globalization. Exploring this era provides insights into the dynamics of power, social change, and the interplay between nations and cultures.

Question: What were the leading causes and consequences of World War I?

Answer: The main causes of World War I were a complex mix of political alliances, imperialism, militarism, and the assassination of Archduke Franz Ferdinand of Austria-Hungary. The consequences of the war included the redrawing of national boundaries, the collapse of empires, and the emergence of new political ideologies.

Quick Explanation: World War I, which lasted from 1914 to 1918, was triggered by the assassination of Archduke Franz Ferdinand and his wife. However, underlying causes such as the system of alliances, competition for colonial territories, and the arms race among European powers had created a tense atmosphere. The war resulted in the deaths of millions of soldiers and civilians, the collapse of the Austro-Hungarian, Russian, Ottoman, and German empires, and the emergence of new nations in Europe.

Question: *What were the main causes and consequences of the Great Depression?*

> **Answer:** The Great Depression was primarily caused by the stock market crash of 1929, which led to a severe economic downturn. Its consequences included widespread unemployment, poverty, and a loss of confidence in the global economic system.

Quick Explanation: The stock market crash of 1929, commonly referred to as "Black Tuesday," signified the onset of the Great Depression, a global era characterized by significant economic downturn. Factors such as overproduction, unequal distribution of wealth, and speculative practices in the stock market contributed to the crisis. The consequences included mass unemployment, homelessness, bank failures, and a prolonged economic recession lasting throughout the 1930s.

Question: *What were the main causes and outcomes of World War II?*

> **Answer:** World War II was primarily caused by the aggressive expansionist policies of Nazi Germany, fascist Italy, and militarist Japan, as well as unresolved issues from World War I. The outcomes of the war included the defeat of the Axis powers, the establishment of the United Nations, and the beginning of the Cold War.

Quick Explanation: World War II, which lasted from 1939 to 1945, was triggered by Germany's invasion of Poland and subsequent acts of aggression. The war involved major global powers and resulted in the deaths of millions of people, including those lost in the Holocaust. The Allies, led by the United States, Soviet Union, and Great Britain, ultimately defeated the Axis powers. The war's aftermath led to the division of Europe, the emergence of the United States and the Soviet Union as superpowers, and the start of the Cold War.

Question: *What were the main causes and consequences of the Civil Rights Movement in the United States?*

> **Answer:** The leading causes of the Civil Rights Movement were racial segregation, discrimination, and the denial of basic rights to African Americans. The consequences included the dismantling of legal segregation, the enactment of civil rights legislation, and the empowerment of marginalized communities.

Quick Explanation: The Civil Rights Movement, which gained momentum in the 1950s and 1960s, aimed to secure equal rights and opportunities for African Americans. Led by figures like Martin Luther King Jr., Rosa Parks, and Malcolm X, the movement challenged racial segregation and fought for voting rights, access to education, and an end to discriminatory practices. As a result of the movement's endeavors, pivotal legislation, such as the Civil Rights Act of 1964 and the Voting Rights Act of 1965, was enacted. These laws played a vital role in ending segregation and safeguarding the rights of minority groups.

Question: *What were the main causes and consequences of the Cold War?*

> **Answer:** The Cold War was primarily caused by ideological differences and power struggles between the United States and the Soviet Union following World War II. Its consequences included the division of Europe, the arms race, and proxy wars fought in various regions of the world.

Quick Explanation: The Cold War refers to the geopolitical tensions and ideological conflict that emerged between the United States and the Soviet Union after World War II. The two superpowers represented contrasting political and economic systems (capitalism vs. communism) and engaged in a prolonged standoff characterized by political, economic, and military competition. The division of Europe into Western and Eastern blocs, the arms race, and proxy conflicts such as the Korean War and the Vietnam War were among the major consequences of the Cold War.

Question: What were the main causes and consequences of the Women's Rights Movement?

Answer: The leading causes of the Women's Rights Movement were gender inequality, discrimination, and the denial of basic rights to women. The consequences included advancing women's rights, changes in societal norms, and increased opportunities for women in various fields.

Quick Explanation: The Women's Rights Movement emerged in the 19th and 20th centuries as a response to the unequal treatment and limited rights afforded to women. Activists such as Susan B. Anthony, Elizabeth Cady Stanton, and Gloria Steinem fought for women's suffrage, equal pay, reproductive rights, and an end to gender discrimination. The movement led to significant achievements, including the ratification of the 19th Amendment (granting women the right to vote), increased participation of women in the workforce, and the establishment of laws to protect women's rights.

Question: What were the main causes and consequences of the Civil War?

Answer: The main cause of the Civil War was the issue of slavery and its expansion into new territories. The consequences included the abolition of slavery, the preservation of the Union, and the reshaping of the United States.

Quick Explanation: The Civil War, fought from 1861 to 1865, was primarily driven by the divide between the Northern states (Union) and the Southern states (Confederacy) over the institution of slavery. The war resulted in the emancipation of enslaved individuals through the Emancipation Proclamation, the preservation of the Union, and the establishment of the Thirteenth Amendment, which abolished slavery. The war also had profound social and economic consequences, including the reconstruction of the South and the reintegration of Confederate states into the Union.

Question: What were the biggest causes and outcomes of the Industrial Revolution?

Answer: The main causes of the Industrial Revolution were advancements in technology, the growth of capitalism, and changes in agricultural practices. The outcomes included urbanization, mass production, and the rise of modern industrialized society.

Quick Explanation: The Industrial Revolution, which occurred from the late 18th to the early 19th century, marked a significant shift from agrarian-based economies to industrialized societies. Key factors driving this transformation included the invention of new machines and technologies, the expansion of factories, and the development of transportation and communication systems. The outcomes of the Industrial Revolution included urbanization, the emergence of a working class, the mass production of goods, and profound social and economic changes.

4.1.7 Integrated Civics - Geography

Geography plays a crucial role in understanding the world and its diverse landscapes, cultures, and resources. In the context of integrated civics, studying geography allows us to explore the physical and human aspects of different regions, understand the interconnectedness of nations, and appreciate the environmental challenges we face.

Question: *What city is the capital of the U.S.?*

Answer: The capital of the United States is Washington, D.C.

Quick Explanation: Washington, D.C., located on the east coast of the United States, is the capital and political center of the country. It is home to the White House, the Capitol Building, and many national monuments and museums.

Question: *What is the longest river in the United States?*

Answer: The longest river in the United States is the Missouri River.

Quick Explanation: The Missouri River stretches approximately 2,341 miles (3,767 kilometers) from its headwaters in the Rocky Mountains to its confluence with the Mississippi River. It passes through several states, including Montana, North Dakota, South Dakota, Nebraska, Iowa, Kansas, and Missouri.

Question: *Which Mountain range is in the western United States?*

Answer: The Rocky Mountains are in the western United States.

Quick Explanation: The Rocky Mountains extend over 3,000 miles (4,800 kilometers) from Canada to New Mexico, traversing several states, including Montana, Idaho, Wyoming, Colorado, and New Mexico. They are known for their breathtaking peaks, diverse wildlife, and recreational opportunities.

Question: *What is the largest national park in the United States?*

Answer: Wrangell-St. Elias National Park and Preserve in Alaska.

Quick Explanation: The largest national park in the United States is Wrangell-St. Elias National Park and Preserve in Alaska. It spans over 13.2 million acres, making it larger than several U.S. states. The park is known for its massive glaciers, towering mountain peaks, and a diverse range of wildlife.

Question: *What is the tallest mountain in the United States?*

Answer: Mount Denali (formerly known as Mount McKinley)

Quick Explanation: Mount Denali (formerly known as Mount McKinley) is the tallest mountain in the United States. It's located in Alaska and has an elevation of 20,310 feet (6,190 meters) above sea level.

Question: *What is the largest lake in the United States?*

Answer: The Lake Superior

Quick Explanation: Lake Superior is the largest lake by surface area in the United States. It is one of the five Great Lakes of North America and spans an area of about 31,700 square miles (82,100 square kilometers).

Question: *"What is the most populous city in the United States?"*

Answer: New York City

Quick Explanation: New York City, often simply referred to as New York, is the most populous city in the United States, with an estimated population of over 8 million people.

Question: What is the largest desert in the United States?

Answer: The Great Basin Desert

Quick Explanation: The largest desert in the United States is the Great Basin Desert. It spans several states, including Nevada, Utah, California, Idaho, and Oregon. It's a cold desert, characterized by its wide temperature fluctuations between day and night, as well as between seasons. The Great Basin Desert covers an area of about 190,000 square miles (492,000 square kilometers).

Question: Which countries border the United States?

Answer: Canada and Mexico

Quick Explanation: The United States shares land borders with two countries. Canada to the north: This is the longest international land border in the world, stretching over 5,525 miles (8,891 kilometers). Mexico to the south: This border is approximately 1,954 miles (3,145 kilometers) long.

Question: What is the oldest national park in the United States?

Answer: Yellowstone National Park.

Quick Explanation: It was established on March 1, 1872, making it the first national park in the U.S. and often considered the first in the world. Located primarily in the state of Wyoming but also extending into Montana and Idaho, Yellowstone is renowned for its geothermal features, especially its geysers, such as Old Faithful, as well as its diverse wildlife.

4.1.8 Integrated Civics - Symbols

Symbols play a significant role in expressing and representing the values, history, and identity of a nation. In integrated civics, studying symbols allows us to understand the cultural significance and symbolism associated with various national emblems, landmarks, and icons. These symbols are powerful reminders of a nation's heritage, values, and aspirations.

Question: What is the national bird of the United States?

Answer: The national bird of the United States is the bald eagle.

Quick Explanation: The bald eagle, with its majestic appearance and strong symbolism, has been the national bird of the United States since 1782. It represents freedom, strength, and independence and is often associated with patriotism and the country's natural beauty.

Question: What does the Statue of Liberty symbolize?

Answer: The Statue of Liberty symbolizes freedom and democracy.

Quick Explanation: The Statue of Liberty, located in New York Harbor, is a universal symbol of freedom and democracy. It was a gift from France to the United States and served as a welcoming symbol to immigrants arriving in America. The statue represents enlightenment, opportunity, and the ideals of liberty and justice.

Question: What is the significance of the American flag's colors?

Answer: The red, white, and blue colors of the American flag symbolize valor, purity, and justice, respectively.

Quick Explanation: The American flag's colors hold symbolic meaning. Red represents valor and bravery, white represents purity and innocence, and blue represents justice and perseverance. These colors embody the values and ideals of the United States.

Question: What does the Liberty Bell symbolize?

Answer: The Liberty Bell symbolizes American independence and the struggle for freedom.

Quick Explanation: The Liberty Bell, located in Philadelphia, Pennsylvania, is an iconic symbol of American independence. It represents the struggle for freedom and equality and is closely associated with the Declaration of Independence and the American Revolutionary War.

Question: What does the Great Seal of the United States depict?

Answer: The Great Seal of the United States depicts an eagle, a shield, and various symbols representing the country's values and heritage.

Quick Explanation: The Great Seal of the United States consists of an eagle clutching a shield, symbolizing the nation's strength and protection. The shield is adorned with thirteen stripes, representing the original thirteen colonies. The seal also includes other symbols, such as an olive branch (symbolizing peace) and arrows (symbolizing readiness for war), along with a banner displaying the motto "E Pluribus Unum" (Out of many, one).

Question: What is the significance of the Lincoln Memorial?

Answer: The Lincoln Memorial honors President Abraham Lincoln and symbolizes his contributions to the preservation of the United States and the abolition of slavery.

Quick Explanation: The Lincoln Memorial, located in Washington, D.C., is a monument dedicated to President Abraham Lincoln. It symbolizes his leadership during a critical period in American history, including his role in preserving the Union and emancipating enslaved individuals. The memorial represents the ideals of freedom, equality, and justice.

Question: What does the national flower of the United States, the rose, symbolize?

Answer: The rose symbolizes love, beauty, and passion.

Quick Explanation: The rose, as the national flower of the United States, holds symbolic significance. It represents love, beauty, and passion and is often associated with emotions, romance, and admiration. The rose's elegance and fragrance make it a cherished symbol in American culture.

Question: What does the White House symbolize?

Answer: The White House symbolizes the executive branch of the United States government and serves as the official residence and workplace of the President.

Quick Explanation: The White House, located in Washington, D.C., is not only the official residence of the President of the United States but also a symbol of the executive branch of government. It represents the power, authority, and decision-making of the President and serves as a historic landmark and symbol of democracy.

Question: What does the Liberty Statue symbolize in France?

> **Answer:** The Liberty Statue, also known as the Marianne, symbolizes freedom, equality, and the French Republic.

Quick Explanation: The Liberty Statue, or Marianne, is an iconic symbol in France. It represents the French Republic and symbolizes the values of freedom, equality, and brotherhood. The statue, with its strong association with the French Revolution, stands as a powerful symbol of French identity and the ideals of liberty.

Question: What is the motto inscribed on the Great Seal of the United States?

> **Answer:** E pluribus unum

Quick Explanation: The motto inscribed on the Great Seal of the United States is "E pluribus unum," which is Latin for "Out of many, one." This phrase reflects the idea that out of many states (or colonies) emerges a single nation. It has been an enduring symbol of the unity and diversity of the United States.

4.1.9 Integrated Civics - Holidays

Holidays play a significant role in the cultural fabric of a nation, serving as occasions to commemorate historical events, celebrate traditions, and foster a sense of unity among its citizens. In the context of integrated civics, understanding the meaning, significance, and observance of different holidays is crucial in appreciating the diverse heritage and shared values of a society. In this section, we will explore integrated civics - holidays by examining ten questions that delve into the traditions, history, and cultural importance of various holidays in the United States. Each question will be followed by its answer and a quick explanation to provide a comprehensive understanding of the topic.

Question: What holiday is celebrated on July 4th in the United States?

> **Answer:** Independence Day is celebrated on July 4th in the United States.

Quick Explanation: Independence Day commemorates the adoption of the Declaration of Independence on July 4, 1776, which declared the United States' independence from Great Britain. It is a national holiday celebrated with fireworks, parades, barbecues, and various patriotic activities.

Question: What is the significance of Thanksgiving Day?

> **Answer:** Thanksgiving Day is a holiday to express gratitude for the blessings of the year and to commemorate the historic harvest feast celebrated by the Pilgrims and Native Americans.

Quick Explanation: Thanksgiving Day is observed on the fourth Thursday of November. It is a time for families and friends to come together, express gratitude, and enjoy a bountiful meal. The holiday has historical roots in the harvest feast shared by the Pilgrims and Native Americans in Plymouth, Massachusetts, in 1621.

Question: What is the meaning of Memorial Day?

> **Answer:** Memorial Day is a day to honor and remember the men and women who died while serving in the U.S. military.

Quick Explanation: Memorial Day, observed on the last Monday in May, is a solemn holiday dedicated to honoring the sacrifices of those who lost their lives while serving in the armed forces. It is a time for reflection, remembrance, and gratitude for the service and sacrifices made to protect the nation.

Question: Which holiday is celebrated on the second Monday in October to commemorate Christopher Columbus's arrival in the Americas?

Answer: Columbus Day is celebrated on the second Monday in October.

Quick Explanation: Columbus Day commemorates Christopher Columbus's arrival in the Americas on October 12, 1492. It recognizes his role in the historical exploration and European contact with the American continents. However, the holiday also sparks discussions about the impact of European colonization on indigenous peoples.

Question: What is the significance of Martin Luther King Jr. Day?

Answer: Martin Luther King Jr. Day commemorates the life and legacy of Dr. Martin Luther King Jr., recognizing his significant contributions to the civil rights movement in the United States.

Quick Explanation: Martin Luther King Jr. Day, observed on the third Monday in January, is a federal holiday that celebrates the achievements and ideals of Dr. Martin Luther King Jr. It serves as a reminder of the ongoing struggle for civil rights, equality, and social justice.

Question: What holiday is dedicated to honoring the achievements and contributions of American workers?

Answer: Labor Day is dedicated to honoring the achievements and contributions of American workers.

Quick Explanation: Labor Day, the first Monday in September, is a holiday that celebrates the contributions and achievements of American workers. It acknowledges the social and economic achievements of the labor movement and the important role that workers play in the nation's prosperity.

Question: Which holiday is celebrated on February 14th as a day to express affection and love?

Answer: Valentine's Day is celebrated on February 14th to express affection and love.

Quick Explanation: Valentine's Day is a holiday associated with expressing love and affection to romantic partners, friends, and family members. It is often celebrated with the exchange of gifts, flowers, and heartfelt messages.

Question: What is the meaning of Veterans Day?

Answer: Veterans Day is a holiday to honor and express gratitude to all military veterans who have served in the United States Armed Forces.

Quick Explanation: Veterans Day, observed on November 11th, honors the service and sacrifice of all military veterans. It is a day to recognize and express gratitude for the bravery, dedication, and contributions of those who have served in the United States Armed Forces.

Question: What holiday is celebrated on December 25th to commemorate the birth of Jesus Christ?

Answer: Christmas is celebrated on December 25th to commemorate the birth of Jesus Christ.

Quick Explanation: Christmas is a religious and cultural holiday that celebrates the birth of Jesus Christ. It is a time for Christians to gather for religious services, exchange gifts, decorate homes, and partake in festive traditions.

Question: Which holiday is observed on the second Monday in February to honor the birthdays of George Washington and Abraham Lincoln?

Answer: Presidents Day is observed on the second Monday in February to honor the birthdays of George Washington and Abraham Lincoln.

Quick Explanation: Presidents Day is a federal holiday that pays tribute to the first President of the United States, George Washington, and the 16th President, Abraham Lincoln. It is a day to recognize the contributions and leadership of past presidents and reflect on the nation's history.

By exploring these questions and their explanations, we gain a deeper understanding of the significance, traditions, and cultural importance of various holidays in the United States. Holidays not only provide opportunities for celebration and reflection but also serve as important markers of history, values, and shared experiences in a diverse society.

Chapter 5: Practical Tests of Civic Education

5.1 Questions from the 2008 Test

The practical tests of civic education assess an individual's knowledge and understanding of important civic concepts and principles. These tests help evaluate an applicant's readiness to become a citizen of the United States. In this chapter, we will focus on the questions from the 2008 version of the civic education test. This version consists of 100 questions covering various aspects of American history, government, and civic responsibilities. We will randomly select ten questions from the list and provide the correct answers at the end. Let's explore these questions and test our knowledge of civic education.

5.1.1 After the First Reading

1. **Question:** What is the supreme law of the land?
2. **Question:** What do we call the first ten amendments to the Constitution?
3. **Question:** What is the economic system in the United States?
4. **Question:** Name one branch or part of the government.
5. **Question:** Who makes federal laws?
6. **Question:** How many U.S. Senators are there?
7. **Question:** What are the two major political parties in the United States?
8. **Question:** How old do citizens have to be to vote for President?
9. **Question:** What is one right or freedom from the First Amendment?
10. **Question:** Who wrote the Declaration of Independence?

Answers

1. The Constitution
2. The Bill of Rights

3. Capitalist economy
4. Legislative
5. Congress
6. One hundred (100)
7. Democratic and Republican
8. Eighteen (18) years old
9. Freedom of speech
10. Thomas Jefferson

In this section, we explored ten random questions from the 2008 civic education test. These questions cover essential aspects of American history, government structure, and civic rights. By answering these questions correctly, applicants demonstrate their understanding of fundamental civic concepts. These practical tests play a crucial role in evaluating an individual's readiness to become a citizen of the United States, ensuring that they have the necessary knowledge to actively participate in the democratic process.

5.1.2 After the Third Reading

1. **Question:** Who is the Chief Justice of the United States now?
2. **Question:** Who is the Governor of your state now?
3. **Question:** What are the two major political parties in the United States?
4. **Question:** What is the capital of your state?
5. **Question:** What is the economic system in the United States?
6. **Question:** What are two parts of the United States Congress?
7. **Question:** What is the supreme law of the land?
8. **Question:** What did the Emancipation Proclamation do?
9. **Question:** What did Susan B. Anthony do?
10. **Question:** What is one reason colonists came to America?

Answers

1. John G. Roberts Jr.
2. [Name of the current governor of your state]
3. Democratic and Republican
4. [Name of the capital city of your state]
5. Capitalist economy
6. Senate and House of Representatives
7. The Constitution
8. Freed the slaves
9. Fought for women's rights
10. Freedom of religion

These ten questions further tested our knowledge of the American government, history, and important figures. By answering these questions correctly, individuals demonstrate their understanding of key civic concepts and their commitment to being informed and engaged citizens. The 2008 civic education test serves as a valuable tool in assessing an individual's readiness to become a citizen of the United States, ensuring that they have the necessary knowledge to actively participate in the democratic process.

By studying and preparing for the civic education test, aspiring citizens can deepen their understanding of American history, government, and civic rights. This knowledge empowers them to contribute positively to their communities and actively engage in the democratic processes that shape the nation.

5.1.3 After the Fifth Reading

After the fifth reading, let's test our knowledge further with ten random questions from the list of 100 questions in the 2008 civic education test. These questions will cover a range of topics related to American history, government, and civic responsibilities. In the end, we will provide the correct answers for each question. Let's begin!

1. **Question:** What are the two major political parties in the United States?
2. **Question:** What is the economic system in the United States?
3. **Question:** What are the first three words of the Constitution?
4. **Question:** What did the Emancipation Proclamation do?
5. **Question:** What is the capital of the United States?
6. **Question:** Who wrote the Declaration of Independence?
7. **Question:** What is the supreme law of the land?
8. **Question:** What did Susan B. Anthony do?
9. **Question:** What is the rule of law?
10. **Question:** What did the United States fight for in World War II?

Answers

1. Democratic and Republican
2. Capitalist economy
3. We the People
4. Freed the slaves
5. Washington, D.C.
6. Thomas Jefferson
7. The Constitution
8. Fought for women's rights
9. Everyone must follow the law, including leaders
10. Freedom and to stop the spread of fascism

These ten questions have challenged our knowledge of American history, government, and civic principles. By correctly answering these questions, individuals demonstrate their understanding of fundamental concepts that underpin the nation's governance and values. The 2008 civic education test plays a vital role in assessing an individual's readiness to become a citizen, ensuring that they possess the necessary knowledge to actively participate in the democratic process and contribute to the nation's well-being.

Studying for the civic education test allows aspiring citizens to delve deeper into the rich tapestry of American history, government structures, and the rights and responsibilities of citizenship. This knowledge empowers individuals to make informed decisions, engage in meaningful civic participation, and contribute positively to the diverse fabric of American society.

By familiarizing themselves with the questions and answers from the 2008 civic education test, individuals can gain a comprehensive understanding of the principles that govern the United States. This understanding not only aids in passing the test but also fosters a sense of civic duty and a commitment to upholding the values and ideals upon which the nation was built.

5.2 Questions from the 2020 Test

This chapter focuses on the questions from the 2020 Civic Education Test. These questions cover various aspects of American history, government systems, rights, and responsibilities.

The 2020 Civic Education Test is designed to assess applicants' knowledge and comprehension of crucial civic topics. The questions encompass a wide range of subjects, including the structure of the government, historical events, constitutional rights, and civic duties. By successfully answering these questions, individuals demonstrate their commitment to becoming informed and engaged citizens.

5.2.1 After the First Reading

1. **Question:** What is one right or freedom from the First Amendment?
2. **Question:** What is the economic system in the United States?
3. **Question:** What is the "rule of law"?
4. **Question:** Who is the Chief Justice of the United States now?
5. **Question:** What is the name of the Speaker of the House of Representatives now?
6. **Question:** How many justices are on the Supreme Court?
7. **Question:** Who wrote the Declaration of Independence?
8. **Question:** Who is the Governor of your state now?
9. **Question:** What is the capital of your state?
10. **Question:** What did Susan B. Anthony do?
11. **Question:** What is one promise you make when you become a United States citizen?
12. **Question:** When do we celebrate Independence Day?

Answers:

1. Freedom of speech
2. Capitalist economy
3. Everyone must follow the law
4. John Roberts
5. Nancy Pelosi
6. Nine
7. Thomas Jefferson
8. State-specific answer required
9. State-specific answer required
10. Fought for women's rights
11. To give up loyalty to other countries
12. July 4th

5.2.2 After the Third Reading

1. **Question:** What are the two rights in the Declaration of Independence?
2. **Question:** What is the economic system in the United States?
3. **Question:** Who is the Commander-in-Chief of the military?

4. **Question:** What is one power of the federal government?
5. **Question:** What is the name of the President of the United States now?
6. **Question:** What did the Emancipation Proclamation do?
7. **Question:** Who did the United States fight in World War II?
8. **Question:** What is the capital of the United States?
9. **Question:** Who wrote the Federalist Papers?
10. **Question:** What are the two rights of everyone living in the United States?
11. **Question:** What is one reason colonists came to America?
12. **Question:** What did the Civil Rights Act of 1964 do?

Answers:
1. Life and liberty
2. Capitalist economy
3. The President
4. Print money
5. Joe Biden
6. Freed the slaves
7. Germany, Japan, and Italy
8. Washington, D.C.
9. James Madison, Alexander Hamilton, and John Jay
10. Freedom of speech and freedom of religion
11. Freedom
12. Outlawed discrimination based on religion, color, race, sex, or national origin

5.2.3 After the Fifth Reading
1. **Question:** What did the Emancipation Proclamation do?
2. **Question:** What is the supreme law of the land?
3. **Question:** What is the economic system in the United States?
4. **Question:** What is one power of the federal government?
5. **Question:** Who is the Chief Justice of the United States now?
6. **Question:** Who is the Governor of your state now?
7. **Question:** What are the two rights in the Declaration of Independence?
8. **Question:** What is the capital of your state?
9. **Question:** What did Susan B. Anthony do?
10. **Question:** When do we celebrate Independence Day?
11. **Question:** Who did the United States fight in World War II?
12. **Question:** What is one promise you make when you become a United States citizen?

Answers:
1. Freed the slaves
2. The Constitution
3. Capitalist economy
4. Print money
5. John Roberts
6. State-specific answer required

7. Life and the Pursuit of Happiness
8. State-specific answer required
9. Fought for women's rights
10. July 4th
11. Germany, Japan, and Italy
12. To give up loyalty to other countries

These questions from the 2020 civic education test have tested our knowledge on a range of important topics. By answering these questions correctly, individuals demonstrate their understanding of key principles, historical events, and governmental structures of the United States. The civic education test plays a crucial role in assessing an individual's readiness to become a citizen and actively participate in the democratic process.

Studying and familiarizing oneself with the questions and answers from the 2020 civic education test allows individuals to acquire a comprehensive understanding of the rights, responsibilities, and values of the United States. This knowledge empowers individuals to become informed citizens who can actively contribute to the country's progress and engage in meaningful civic participation.

By consistently reviewing and practicing these questions, individuals can enhance their civic knowledge, deepen their understanding of American history and government, and strengthen their commitment to upholding the principles and ideals of the United States. The civic education test serves as a pathway for individuals to fully embrace their roles as responsible and engaged citizens, ensuring the continued strength and prosperity of the nation.

Conclusion

The *US Citizenship Test Study Guide 2023/2024* is a comprehensive and invaluable resource for individuals preparing to become citizens of the United States. Throughout its pages, it provides a wealth of knowledge, insights, and practical examples to help applicants succeed in the citizenship test and, more importantly, develop a deep understanding of American history, government systems, and civic responsibilities.

By studying this guide, aspiring citizens can embark on their journey with confidence, knowing they are equipped with the necessary tools to navigate the complexities of the naturalization process. The guide offers clear explanations and concise answers to a wide range of questions, ensuring that applicants can verify their understanding and address any knowledge gaps effectively.

The study guide focuses on the practical aspects of the citizenship test and emphasizes the importance of active citizenship and civic engagement. It encourages applicants to embrace their rights and duties as American citizens and actively participate in the democratic processes that shape the nation. By providing insights into the principles of American democracy, historical events, and key civic concepts, the guide fosters a sense of civic responsibility and empowers individuals to make their own decisions and contribute meaningfully to their communities.

Moreover, the guide recognizes the significance of language proficiency in the naturalization process. It provides practical tips, examples, and exercises to help applicants improve their English language skills, enabling effective communication and integration into American society.

The *US Citizenship Test Study Guide 2023/2024* goes beyond being a mere test preparation tool; it serves as a lifelong resource for individuals on their citizenship journey. It equips readers with a solid foundation of knowledge that will continue to be relevant and useful throughout their lives as American citizens. The guide encourages ongoing learning, civic involvement, and an appreciation for the values and principles that define the United States.

In a world where citizenship carries great significance, this book stands as a beacon of knowledge and guidance. It empowers individuals to fulfill the requirements of the citizenship test and become informed, engaged, and active citizens who contribute to the rich tapestry of American society.

As readers delve into the pages of this study guide, they are embarking on a transformative journey — a journey that not only prepares them for the citizenship test but also shapes their understanding of what it means to be an American citizen. With dedication, perseverance, and the guidance offered in this comprehensive resource, individuals can confidently step forward and embrace the rights and duties that come with the honor of being a citizen of the United States of America.

2008 CIVICS TEST

Nos.	Questions	Answers
1	What is the supreme law of the land?	The Constitution
2	What does the Constitution do?	Defines the government Protects basic rights of Americans Sets up the government
3	The idea of self-government is in the first three words of the Constitution. What are these words?	We, the People
4	What is an amendment?	A change (to the Constitution) or An addition (to the Constitution)
5	What do we call the first ten amendments to the Constitution?	The Bill of Rights
6	What is one right or freedom from the First Amendment?	Speech, Religion Assembly Press Petition the government
7	What is the total number of amendments present in the Constitution?	27
8	What did the Declaration of Independence do?	Proclaimed our independence from Great Britain Expressed our declaration of independence from Great Britain Stated that the U.S. has achieved freedom from Great Britain
9	Which two rights are mentioned in the Declaration of Independence?	Life Liberty Pursuit of happiness
10	What is freedom of religion?	You can practice any religion or not practice a religion
11	What is the economic system in the United States?	Capitalist economy Market economy
12	What is the "rule of law"?	Everyone must follow the law Leaders must obey the law Government must obey the law No one is above the law
13	Name one branch or part of the government	Congress Legislative President Executive The courts Judicial
14	What prevents any single branch of government from acquiring excessive power?	Checks and balances Separation of powers

Nos.	Questions	Answers
15	Who holds the authority in the executive branch?	The President
16	Who makes federal laws?	Congress Senate and House of Representatives U.S. or national legislature
17	What are the two components that make up the U.S. Congress?	The Senate and House of Representatives
18	What is the total number of U.S. senators?	100
19	For how many years does a U.S. senator serve?	6
20	Who is currently one of your state's U.S. senators?	The answer will vary based on where the applicant lives
21	The House of Representatives has how many voting members?	435
22	For how many years does a U.S. representative serve?	2
23	Name your U.S. representative.	The answer will vary based on where the applicant lives
24	Whom does a U.S. senator represent?	All people in the state
25	Why do some states have more representatives than other states?	Because of the state's population Because they have more people Because some states have more people
26	We elect a president to serve for how many years?	4
27	In what month do we vote for a president?	November
28	What is the name of the President of the United States now?	Joe Biden
29	Who currently holds the position of Vice President of the United States?	Kamala Harris
30	If the President is unable to continue serving, who assumes the role of the President?	The Vice President
31	If both the President and Vice President are unable to continue serving, who assumes the role of the President?	The Speaker of the House
32	Who is the Commander in Chief of the military?	The President
33	Who signs bills to become laws?	The President
34	Who vetoes bills?	The President
35	What does the President's Cabinet do?	Advises the President

Nos.	Questions	Answers
36	Name two Cabinet-level positions	Secretary of Agriculture Secretary of Commerce Secretary of Defense Secretary of Education Secretary of Energy Secretary of Health and Human Services Secretary of Homeland Security Secretary of Housing and Urban Development Secretary of the Interior Secretary of Labor Secretary of State Secretary of Transportation Secretary of the Treasury Secretary of Veterans Affairs Attorney General Vice President
37	What does the judicial branch do?	Decides if a law goes against the Constitution, Explains laws Resolves disputes (disagreements) Reviews laws
38	What is the highest court in the United States?	The Supreme Court
39	How many justices are on the Supreme Court?	Nine justices
40	Who currently holds the position of Chief Justice of the United States?	John Roberts
41	Name one power of the federal government.	To print money To declare war To create an army To make treaties
42	Name one power of the states.	Approve zoning and land use Give a driver's license Provide protection (police) Provide safety (fire departments) Provide schooling and education
43	Who is the governor of your state now?	The answer will vary based on where the applicant lives
44	What is the capital of your state?	The answer will vary based on where the applicant lives
45	Name two major political parties in the United States.	Democratic and Republican
46	What is the political party of the President now?	Democratic Party
47	Who currently holds the position of Speaker of the House of Representatives?	Kevin McCarthy

Nos.	Questions	Answers
48	Describe one of the four amendments to the Constitution about who can vote.	Individuals of any gender and race, who are citizens, have the right to vote Every citizen is eligible to vote Citizens who are 18 years old or older can vote Voting does not require the payment of a poll tax
49	Name one responsibility that is only for US citizens.	Participate as a juror Exercise the right to vote in federal elections
50	Name one right only for United States citizens.	Vote in a federal election Run for federal office
51	Name two rights of everyone living in the U.S.	Freedom of assembly Freedom of expression Freedom of religion Freedom of speech Freedom to petition the government The right to bear arms
52	What do we express loyalty to when reciting the Pledge of Allegiance?	The United States The flag
53	Name one promise you make when you become a U.S citizen.	Demonstrate loyalty to the United States Defend the Laws and Constitution of the United States Renounce allegiance to any other countries Abide by the laws of the United States Serve the nation by undertaking significant work when necessary Serve in the U.S. military if required
54	What age do citizens have to be to vote for President?	18 and older
55	Name two ways that U.S. citizens can participate in their democracy	Call senators and representatives Give an elected official your opinion on an issue Help with a campaign Join a civic group Join a community group Join a political party Publicly support or oppose an issue or policy Run for office Vote Write to a newspaper
56	What date is the last day you can submit federal income tax forms?	April 15
57	When must all men register for the Selective Service?	At 18 Between 18 and 26
58	Name one reason colonists came to America.	Freedom Political liberty Religious freedom Economic opportunity Practice their religion Escape persecution

Nos.	Questions	Answers
59	Who inhabited America prior to the arrival of Europeans?	Native Americans
60	Which group of people was taken to the U.S and sold as slaves?	Africans People from Africa
61	What was the reason behind the colonists' fight against the British?	Due to excessive taxes imposed without representation (taxation without representation). Because the British army occupied their homes. Because they didn't have self-government
62	Who wrote the Declaration of Independence?	Thomas Jefferson
63	When was the Declaration of Independence officially adopted?	July 4, 1776
64	Name three of the 13 original states.	New Hampshire Massachusetts Rhode Island Connecticut New York New Jersey Pennsylvania Delaware Maryland Virginia North Carolina South Carolina Georgia
65	What happened at the Constitutional Convention?	The Constitution was written. The Founding Fathers wrote the Constitution.
66	When was the Constitution written?	1787
67	Name one of the writers of the Federalist Papers.	(James) Madison (Alexander) Hamilton (John) Jay Publius
68	Name one thing Benjamin Franklin is famous for?	U.S. diplomat The oldest member of the Constitutional Convention First Postmaster General of the United States Writer of "Poor Richard's Almanac" Started the first free libraries
69	Who is considered the "Father of Our Country"?	(George) Washington
70	Who was the first president?	(George) Washington
71	Which territory did the United States acquire from France in 1803 through a purchase?	The Louisiana Territory Louisiana
72	Name one war fought by the U.S In the 1800s.	Civil War Mexican-American War

Nos.	Questions	Answers
		Spanish-American War War of 1812
73	Name the U.S. war between the North and the South.	The Civil War The War between the States
74	Name one problem that led to the Civil War.	Slavery Economic reasons States' rights
75	Name one important thing that Abraham Lincoln did.	Freed the slaves (Emancipation Proclamation) Saved (or preserved) the Union Led the U.S. during the Civil War
76	What did the Emancipation Proclamation do?	Freed the slaves Freed slaves in the Confederacy Freed slaves in the Confederate states Freed slaves in most Southern states
77	What did Susan B. Anthony do?	Fought for women's rights Fought for civil rights
78	Name one war fought by the United States in the 1900s.	(Persian) Gulf War Korean War Vietnam War World War I World War II
79	Who was President during World War I?	(Woodrow) Wilson
80	Who was President during the Great Depression and World War II?	(Franklin) Roosevelt
81	Who did the United States fight in World War II?	Germany, Japan, and Italy
82	Before he was President, Eisenhower was a general. What war was he in?	World War II
83	During the Cold War, what was the main concern of the United States?	Communism
84	Which movement attempted to put an end to racial discrimination?	Civil Rights Movement
85	What were the accomplishments and contributions of Martin Luther King, Jr.?	Fought for civil rights Worked for equality for all Americans
86	What significant occurrence took place in the United States on September 11, 2001?	Terrorists attacked the United States.
87	Name one Native American tribe in the United States	Cherokee Navajo Sioux Chippewa Choctaw Pueblo Apache Iroquois

Nos.	Questions	Answers
		Creek
		Blackfeet
		Seminole
		Cheyenne
		Arawak
		Shawnee
		Mohegan
		Huron
		Oneida
		Lakota
		Crow
		Teton
		Hopi
		Inuit
88	Provide the name of one of the two longest rivers in the United States.	Mississippi (River) Missouri (River)
89	What ocean is on the West Coast of the U.S.?	Pacific Ocean
90	Which ocean is located along the East Coast of the United States?	Atlantic Ocean
91	Name one U.S. territory.	Puerto Rico U.S. Virgin Islands American Samoa Northern Mariana Islands Guam
92	Name one state that borders Canada.	Maine New Hampshire Vermont New York Pennsylvania Ohio Michigan Minnesota North Dakota Montana Idaho Washington Alaska
93	Name one state that borders Mexico.	Arizona New Mexico California Texas
94	What is the capital of the United States?	Washington, D.C.
95	Where is the Statue of Liberty?	New York Harbor Liberty Island Near New York City On the Hudson River

Nos.	Questions	Answers
96	What is the reason behind the presence of 13 stripes on the flag?	Because the stripes represent the original colonies Because there were 13 original colonies
97	What is the significance of having 50 stars on the flag?	Because each star represents a state Because there are 50 states Because there is one star for each state
98	What is the name of the national anthem?	The Star-Spangled Banner
99	When do we celebrate Independence Day?	July 4th
100	Name two national U.S. holidays.	New Year's Day Martin Luther King, Jr. Day Presidents' Day Memorial Day Independence Day Labor Day Columbus Day Veterans Day Thanksgiving Christmas

2020 CIVICS TEST

No.	Question	Answer
1	What type of government does the United States have?	Constitution-based federal republic Representative democracy Republic
2	What is the significance of the phrase "We the People" at the beginning of the U.S. Constitution?	Popular sovereignty Example of social contract Consent of the governed People should govern themselves Self-government
3	What is the supreme law of the land?	U.S. Constitution
4	Name one thing the U.S. Constitution does.	Defines powers of government Forms the government Defines the parts of government Protects the rights of the people
5	What is the process for amending the United States Constitution?	Amendments The amendment processes
6	What is the purpose of the protections provided by the Bill of Rights?	The basic rights of Americans The basic rights of people living in the United States
7	What is the total number of amendments in the U.S. Constitution?	Twenty-seven (27)
8	What is the significance of the Declaration of Independence?	It says all people are created equal It identifies inherent rights It says America is free from British rule It identifies individual liberties
9	Which foundational document declared the independence of the American colonies from Britain?	Declaration of Independence
10	Please provide two significant concepts found in both the U.S. Constitution and the Declaration of Independence.	Equality Liberty Limited government Natural rights Self-government Social contract
11	In which foundational document can the phrase "Life, Liberty, and the pursuit of Happiness" be found?	Declaration of Independence
12	What is the prevailing economic system in the United States?	Free market economy Capitalism

No.	Question	Answer
13	What is the rule of law?	Everyone must follow the law Leaders must obey the law Government must obey the law No one is above the law
14	The U.S. Constitution was influenced by numerous documents. Please mention one of them.	Anti-Federalist Papers Articles of Confederation Declaration of Independence Federalist Papers Fundamental Orders of Connecticut Iroquois Great Law of Peace Mayflower Compact Virginia Declaration of Rights
15	There are three branches of government. Why?	Checks and balances Separation of powers So that one part does not become too powerful
16	Name the three branches of government.	Congress, the president, and the courts, Legislative, executive, and judicial
17	To which branch of government does the President of the United States belong as the leader?	Executive branch
18	Which branch of the federal government is responsible for creating laws?	U.S. or national legislature U.S. Congress Legislative branch
19	What are the two components that make up the U.S. Congress?	Senate and House (of Representatives)
20	Name one power of the U.S. Congress.	Writes laws Declares war Makes the federal budget
21	How many U.S. senators are there?	One hundred (100)
22	How long is a term for a U.S. senator?	Six (6) years
23	Who is one of your state's U.S. senators now?	Responses will vary. [Residents of the District of Columbia and U.S. territories should indicate that the District of Columbia (or the specific territory) does not have any U.S. senators.]
24	What is the total number of voting members in the House of Representatives?	Four hundred thirty-five (435)
25	What is the duration of a term for the House of Representatives member?	Two (2) years

No.	Question	Answer
26	What is the reason for the difference in the length of terms between U.S. representatives and U.S. senators?	To more closely follow public opinion
27	How many senators does each state in the United States have?	Two (2)
28	What is the reason behind each state having two senators?	Equal representation (for small states) The Great Compromise (Connecticut Compromise)
29	Name your U.S. representative.	Responses may differ. [Residents of territories with nonvoting Delegates or Resident Commissioners may mention the name of their respective Delegate. Alternatively, it is acceptable to state that the territory does not have any voting representatives in Congress.]
30	Who currently holds the position of Speaker of the House of Representatives?	Refer to gov/citizenship/test updates.
31	Who is the constituency represented by a U.S. senator?	Citizens of their state
32	Who has the authority to elect U.S. senators?	Citizens from their state
33	Whom does a member of the House of Representatives represent?	Citizens in their (congressional) district Citizens in their district
34	Who is responsible for electing members of the House of Representatives?	Citizens from their (congressional) district
35	Why do certain states have a greater number of representatives compared to others?	Because of the state's population Some states have more people They have more people
36	How many years is the President of the United States elected for?	Four (4) years
37	What is the rationale behind the limitation that restricts the President of the United States to serving only two terms?	22nd Amendment Limiting presidential power
38	What is the name of the President of the United States now?	Refer to gov/citizenship/test updates for the current President of the United States.
39	Who currently holds the position of the Vice President of the United States?	Check gov/citizenship/test updates for the current Vice President of the United States.

No.	Question	Answer
40	If the President is unable to serve, who assumes the role of the President?	The Vice President (of the United States)
41	Provide one example of a power held by the President.	Chief diplomat Commander in Chief (of the military) Enforces laws Signs bills into law Vetoes bills
42	Who is the Commander in Chief of the U.S. military?	The President (of the United States)
43	Who signs bills to become laws?	The President (of the United States)
44	Who vetoes bills?	The President (of the United States)
45	Who appoints federal judges?	The President (of the United States)
46	The executive branch has many parts. Name one.	President (of the United States) Cabinet Federal departments and agencies
47	What does the President's Cabinet do?	Advises the President (of the United States)
48	What are two Cabinet-level positions?	Attorney General Secretary of Agriculture Secretary of Commerce Secretary of Defense Secretary of Education Secretary of Energy Secretary of Health and Human Services Secretary of Homeland Security Secretary of Housing and Urban Development Secretary of Labor Secretary of State Secretary of the Interior Secretary of the Treasury Secretary of Transportation Secretary of Veterans Affairs Vice President (of the United States)
49	Why is the Electoral College important?	It decides who is elected It offers a middle ground between the direct election of the president and the involvement of Congress.
50	Name one component of the judicial branch.	The Supreme Court Or the Federal Courts
51	What is the role or function of the judicial branch?	Decides if a law goes against the U.S. Constitution Explains laws Resolves disputes about the law Reviews laws

No.	Question	Answer
52	What is the name of the highest court within the United States?	Supreme Court
53	How many positions are there on the Supreme Court?	Nine (9)
54	How many Supreme Court justices are required to decide a case?	Five (5)
55	What is the duration of service for Supreme Court justices?	For life Lifetime appointment Until retirement
56	What is the reason behind Supreme Court justices serving for life?	To be independent of politics To limit outside political influence
57	Who currently holds the position of Chief Justice of the United States?	Check on gov/citizenship/test updates for the name of the Chief Justice of the U.S.
58	Identify one authority exclusive to the federal government.	Create an army Declare war Make treaties Mint coins Print paper money Set foreign policy
59	Name one power that is only for the states.	Approve zoning and land use Give a driver's license Provide protection (police) Provide safety (fire departments) Provide schooling and education
60	What is the intended function or purpose of the 10th Amendment?	Powers not delegated to the federal government are reserved for the states or the people
61	Who holds the position of the governor in your state?	Answers will vary as per the state
62	What is the capital city of the state you are in?	Answers will vary as per the state
63	Out of the four amendments in the U.S. Constitution regarding voting eligibility, explain one of them.	A male citizen of any race can vote Any citizen can vote Citizens eighteen and older can vote You don't have to pay a poll tax to vote
64	Who possesses the right to vote in federal elections, run for federal office, and participate as a juror in the United States?	Any citizens Citizens of the United States

No.	Question	Answer
65	What are the three rights of everyone living in the United States?	Freedom of assembly Freedom of expression Freedom of religion Freedom of speech Freedom to petition the government The right to bear arms
66	To what do we express allegiance when reciting the Pledge of Allegiance?	The flag The United States
67	What are two commitments that individuals make when reciting the Oath of Allegiance as new citizens?	Be loyal to the United States Defend the U.S. Constitution Give up loyalty to other countries Obey the laws of the United States Serve the nation if needed Serve in the military if needed
68	What are the ways in which individuals can obtain United States citizenship?	Be born in the United States Derive citizenship Naturalize
69	Provide two examples of civic engagement or participation in the United States.	Contact elected officials Give an elected official your opinion on an issue Help with a campaign Join a civic group Join a community group Join a political party Run for office Support or oppose an issue or policy Vote Write to a newspaper
70	Name one method through which Americans can contribute to their country.	Obey the law Pay taxes Run for office Serve in the military Vote Work for local state, or federal government
71	What is the significance or importance of paying federal taxes?	All people pay to fund the federal government Civic duty Required by law Required by the U.S. Constitution (16th Amendment)
72	Why is it crucial for males between the ages of 18-25 to register for the Selective Service? Please provide one justification.	Civic duty Makes the draft fair, if needed Required by law

No.	Question	Answer
73	The colonists migrated to America for various motivations. Please mention one.	Economic opportunity Escape persecution Freedom Political liberty Religious freedom
74	Who inhabited America prior to the arrival of Europeans?	Native Americans
75	Which specific group of people was captured, enslaved, and traded as commodities?	Africans People from Africa
76	Which conflict did the Americans engage in to secure their independence from Britain?	American Revolution War for American Independence The American Revolutionary War
77	Provide one justification for the American declaration of independence from Britain.	Boston Massacre British soldiers stayed in Americans' houses (boarding, quartering) Boston Tea Party (Tea Act) High taxes Intolerable (Coercive) Acts Stamp Act Sugar Act Taxation without representation They did not have self-government Townshend Acts
78	Who wrote the Declaration of Independence?	Thomas Jefferson
79	When was the Declaration of Independence adopted?	July 4, 1776
80	The American Revolution had many important events. Name one.	Battle of Bunker Hill Battle of Saratoga Battle of Yorktown (British surrender at Yorktown) Declaration of Independence Valley Forge (Encampment) Washington Crossing the Delaware (Battle of Trenton)
81	There were 13 original states. Name five.	Connecticut Delaware Georgia Maryland Massachusetts New Hampshire New Jersey New York North Carolina

No.	Question	Answer
		Pennsylvania Rhode Island South Carolina Virginia
82	What founding document was written in 1787?	U.S. Constitution
83	The Federalist Papers supported the passage of the U.S. Constitution. Name one of the writers.	James Madison Alexander Hamilton John Jay Publius
84	Why were the Federalist Papers important?	They helped people understand the U.S. Constitution They supported passing the U.S. Constitution
85	Benjamin Franklin is famous for many things. Name one.	Founded the first free public libraries First Postmaster General of the United States Helped write the Declaration of Independence Inventor U.S. diplomat
86	George Washington is famous for many things. Name one.	"Father of Our Country" The first president of the United States General of the Continental Army President of the Constitutional Convention
87	Thomas Jefferson is famous for many things. Name one.	Writer of the Declaration of Independence The third president of the United States Doubled the size of the United States (Louisiana Purchase) First Secretary of State Founded the University of Virginia Writer of the Virginia Statute on Religious Freedom
88	James Madison is famous for many things. Name one.	"Father of the Constitution" The fourth president of the United States President during the War of 1812 One of the writers of the Federalist Papers
89	Alexander Hamilton is famous for many things. Name one.	First Secretary of the Treasury One of the writers of the Federalist Papers Helped establish the First Bank of the United States An aide to General George Washington Member of the Continental Congress
90	What territory did the United States buy from France in 1803?	Louisiana Territory Louisiana
91	Name one war fought by the United States in the 1800s.	War of 1812 Mexican-American War Civil War Spanish-American War

No.	Question	Answer
92	Name the U.S. war between the North and the South.	The Civil War
93	The Civil War had many important events. Name one.	(Battle of) Fort Sumter Emancipation Proclamation (Battle of) Vicksburg (Battle of) Gettysburg Sherman's March (Surrender at) Appomattox (Battle of) Antietam/Sharpsburg
94	Abraham Lincoln is famous for many things. Name one.	Freed the slaves (Emancipation Proclamation) Saved (or preserved) the Union Led the United States during the Civil War 16th president of the United States Delivered the Gettysburg Address
95	What did the Emancipation Proclamation do?	Freed the slaves Freed slaves in the Confederacy Freed slaves in the Confederate states Freed slaves in most Southern states
96	What U.S. war ended slavery?	The Civil War
97	What amendment gives citizenship to all persons born in the United States?	14th Amendment
98	When did all men get the right to vote?	After the Civil War During Reconstruction (With the) 15th Amendment 1870
99	Name one leader of the women's rights movement in the 1800s.	Susan Anthony Elizabeth Cady Stanton Sojourner Truth Harriet Tubman Lucretia Mott Lucy Stone
100	Name one war fought by the United States in the 1900s.	World War I World War II Korean War Vietnam War (Persian) Gulf War
101	Why did the United States enter World War I?	Because Germany attacked U.S. (civilian) ships To support the Allied Powers (England, France, Italy, and Russia) To oppose the Central Powers (Germany, Austria-Hungary, the Ottoman Empire, and Bulgaria)

No.	Question	Answer
102	When did all women get the right to vote?	1920 After World War I (With the) 19th Amendment
103	What was the Great Depression?	Longest economic recession in modern history
104	When did the Great Depression start?	The Great Crash (1929) The stock market crash of 1929
105	Who was president during the Great Depression and World War II?	(Franklin) Roosevelt
106	Why did the United States enter World War II?	(Bombing of) Pearl Harbor Japanese attacked Pearl Harbor To support the Allied Powers (England, France, and Russia) To oppose the Axis Powers (Germany, Italy, and Japan)
107	Dwight Eisenhower is famous for many things. Name one.	General during World War II President at the end of (during) the Korean War 34th president of the United States Signed the Federal-Aid Highway Act of 1956 (Created the Interstate System)
108	Who was the United States' main rival during the Cold War?	Soviet Union USSR Russia
109	During the Cold War, what was one main concern of the United States?	Communism Nuclear war
110	Why did the United States enter the Korean War?	To stop the spread of communism
111	Why did the United States enter the Vietnam War?	To stop the spread of communism
112	What did the civil rights movement do?	Fought to end racial discrimination
113	Martin Luther King, Jr. is famous for many things. Name one.	Fought for civil rights Worked for equality for all Americans Worked to ensure that people would "not be judged by the color of their skin but by the content of their character."
114	Why did the United States enter the Persian Gulf War?	To force the Iraqi military from Kuwait

No.	Question	Answer
115	What major event happened on September 11, 2001, in the United States?	Terrorists attacked the United States Terrorists took over two planes and crashed them into the World Trade Center in New York City Terrorists took over a plane and crashed into the Pentagon in Arlington, Virginia Terrorists took over a plane originally aimed at Washington, DC. and crashed in a field in Pennsylvania
116	Name one U.S. military conflict after the September 11, 2001 attacks.	(Global) War on Terror War in Afghanistan War in Iraq
117	Name one Native American tribe in the United States.	Apache Blackfeet Cayuga Cherokee Cheyenne Chippewa Choctaw Creek Crow Hopi Huron Inupiat Lakota Mohawk Mohegan Navajo Oneida Onondaga Pueblo Seminole Seneca Shawnee Sioux Teton Tuscarora
118	Name one example of American innovation.	Light bulb Automobile (cars, combustible engine) Skyscrapers Airplane Assembly line Landing on the moon Integrated circuit (IC)
119	What is the capital of the United States?	Washington, D.C.

No.	Question	Answer
120	Where is the Statue of Liberty?	New York (Harbor) Liberty Island [Also acceptable are, near New York City, and on the Hudson (River).]
121	Why does the flag have 13 stripes?	(Because there were) 13 original colonies (Because of the stripes) represent the original colonies
122	Why does the flag have 50 stars?	(Because there is) one star for each state (Because) each star represents a state (Because there are) 50 states
123	What is the name of the national anthem?	The Star-Spangled Banner
124	The Nation's first motto was "E Pluribus Unum. What does that mean?	Out of many, one We all become one
125	What is Independence Day?	A holiday to celebrate U.S. independence (from Britain) The country's birthday
126	Name three national U.S. holidays.	New Year's Day Martin Luther King, Day Presidents Day (Washington's Birthday) Memorial Day Independence Day Labor Day Columbus Day Veterans Day Thanksgiving Day Christmas Day
127	What is Memorial Day?	A holiday to honor soldiers who died in military service
128	What is Veterans Day?	A holiday to honor people in the (U.S.) military A holiday to honor people who have served (in the U.S. military)

Made in the USA
Monee, IL
02 January 2024

50939489R00070